Gerald Lee Wall

GOD'S BINARY CODE

The Bible and Nature Reveal God's Hidden Code to Man

ISBN: 9798617783768

Cover Design and Layout by Gerald Lee Wall

geraldwall@mail.com

*All scripture is from the King James Version
unless otherwise specified!

Dedication

To **all** the true **Believers**, who love the truth, search for it, and manifest its light in a dark world! To the **Son**, who has *redeemed* us by his **blood** through grace and mercy, and who leaves the flock to seek out the one. To the **Spirit** who dwells within the redeemed to lead and **guide** them into all **truth** and is their Comforter in a harsh fallen world. And to the **Father** of lights who created us and has prepared an eternal home for us. **Praise** be to the only **true** and Living **God!**

Preface

Although the Bible is infallible in its original language all English translations have minor textual errors. I do not believe these alter the spiritual conveyance or meaning, but the original Hebrew and Greek text can often have multiple synonyms and word variations. Some translations are better for doctrine and study, while others for preaching and conversing. I mostly use the King James Version because of familiarity but I have used other translations here only because some speak clearer to the subject at hand. The following is the translation references used in this book

(NIV) - New International version
(NAS) - New American Standard
(ESV) - English Standard Version
(NKJV) - New King James Version
(HCSB) - Holman Christian Standard Bible

The purpose of this book is to break things down into its simplest forms. Pay great attention to the usage of **Bold type** in each paragraph because it is not only for emphasis but also displays much of the **duality** of the subject!

This is not a book of Theology or doctrine but rather it uses symbolism and biblical patterns to convey spiritual truths! As with God's word, it is important to pray as to what is to be taken figuratively and what is literal. You may not agree with some of it but as an old preacher once told me "Just eat the **meat** and spit out the **bones**!"

Enjoy!

Table of Contents

Table of Contents (Continued)

Table of Contents (Continued)

Table of Contents (Continued)

Introduction

God has a **code** that He has put into all creation. It is revealed in the Bible and confirmed in nature and it is a principle often seen in science! It is a simple **syntax** that explains our existence, as well as governs and defines our lives. The evidence of a Creator is not only revealed in the **complexity of what** has been made, but also in the **simplicity of why** we are made. The binary code is both surprisingly illusive and yet amazingly simple. It is divinely designed that way so that the intellectual is blinded to it but the simple minded can see it clearly! Jesus said that it is something which is both **hidden** and **revealed**!

"... I thank thee, O Father, Lord of heaven and earth, because thou hast ***hid*** these things from the wise and prudent, and hast ***revealed*** them unto babes." Matthew. 11:25

Another proof of God's code is the fact that the world around is made up of DNA that utilize a simple **language** to communicate intelligent design. God has encoded His fingerprint into all that He has made. He has placed in living material not a random jumble of cells, but a carefully complex DNA code that can replicate itself as well as heal injured cells over time. The vast **complexity** of our human body, brains, skeletal system, respiratory system, nervous system, and vascular system can all be broken down into **simple** (or not-so-simple) cells. The belief that living things could of randomly assembled into to such complexity through evolution only proves how God's truth is hidden from the wise and prudent. Science and atheism **deny** the creative power of God, yet **simple faith reveals it**!

"For you ***created*** my inmost being; you knit me together in my mother's womb. I praise you because I am ***fearfully and wonderfully made***; your works are wonderful." Psalm 139:13,14 (NIV)

The key to understanding this **binary code** is to break things down to its most simplistic state. Binary means **two systems**. The dictionary defines it as ***"relating to, composed of, or involving two things.***

Introduction (Continued)

Nearly everything in the physical world that is **matter** can be broken down into **atoms** which can then be broken down into subatomic **particles** of two things: a **nucleus** (protons and neutrons) **and electrons.** One is **central** and the other is **separated** but within its orbit! The binary system is often composed of **opposing** forces and sometimes complementary forces. The inner sub-atomic particle has a neutral and positive charge and the outer electron has a negative charge. Together they work in tandem, but apart they can cause a nuclear bomb!

The binary code in matter is the **two-phase system** that, by all means, should cancel itself out, yet somehow it binds itself together to form the building blocks of everything that is made. These elements should repel each other, but somehow, they hold together. The bible says:

> "For in him all things were created: things in heaven and on earth, visible and invisible, whether thrones or powers or rulers or authorities; all things have been created through him and for him. He is before all things, and ***in him all things hold together.***" Colossians 1:16-17 (NIV)

Many of the **forces** around us are binary systems. **Electricity** is a binary system. A car **battery** has **positive** and **negative** terminals. When you put battery cables on it and touch the ends, there will be a spark or discharge of energy.

Magnetism also has a **positive** and a **negative** charge. Like charges will attract but **unlike** charges will repel. This is a simple example of the world around us that engages **contrary and opposing forces** that are often pulling us into **two** directions.

Many physicists now talk about matter and dark matter or antimatter, strong forces and weak forces; energy and dark energy. Not only have we discovered new forces but opposing forces.

A computer is a very sophisticated yet powerfully complex machine that uses variations of **code languages. These languages** enable it to do a multitude of things, such as display photos, enable writing and printing, communicate with a network and interface with the internet, etc. However, when you break up those languages into its simplest form it is called ***Binary code***. This only uses a series of two characters: **ones and zeros**. Amazingly, all computer instructions are based on the combination of these **two numbers**.

The human brain is one of the most complex systems, enabling it to comprehend, calculate, reason, and think and, yet, it too has a binary code. The brain is composed of synapses that allow neurons (nerve cells) to cross gaps between them. It is sort of like someone coming to a **fork in the road** and having to choose the **left or right** or coming to a door and it is either **opened or closed**. Only **two options** are available. This is how the brain works, by making thousands of these decisions at the speed of thought!

Thus, the **pattern** emerges! This is **God's binary code** and it is built into everything we do. Both the physical and the spiritual world around us is comprised of **two opposing options: Satan or God, good or evil, light or dark, right or wrong, heaven or hell, truth or error, and much more.**

The B**ible does not have contradictions,** but **it does have contrasts** and the binary system of the Bible is made up many opposing and contrasting forces, ideas, and principles that show the dual nature of life.

In these pages, we will see the binary world that God has created and how he allows us the free will to ultimately choose one of **two ways, two directions, two morals, two choices and, ultimately and two final destinations!**

Chapter 1 - The Two Divisions - the Code in Creation

The Binary Systems

The 1st Day- Heaven & Earth, Light & Darkness, Night & Day

"In the beginning God created the heaven and the earth. And the earth was without form, and void; and darkness was upon the face of the deep. And the Spirit of God moved upon the face of the waters. And God said, Let there be light: and there was light. And God saw the light, that it was good: and God **divided** the **light from the darkness**. And God called the light **Day**, and the darkness he called **Night**. And the **evening** and the **morning** were the first day" Genesis 1:1-5

On the very ***first day*** of creation when God created the **heaven and earth.** He made a **division**, a **separation,** and a **distinction**. The word "**heaven"** is often translated as "heavens" in the plural because the bible refers to **three heavens** (2 Corinthians 12:2) which many believe are **the atmosphere** over earth, **the starry space** beyond the earth and **the heavenly realm of God** beyond space. Regardless, we see the **first binary creation of two systems**: a **heavenly system** and an **earthly system**. They are totally **unlike** each other yet **complement** each other and **work together** as part of the environment that God would make for man!

After the heavens and the earth were made, God created **light**. Notice that **the bible *never says that God created darkness***. The darkness was already there, created by Satan, but we will discuss that later. What God does is **make a distinction between the light and the darkness** and calls it **day and night**. Keep in mind that God has not created the sun yet, so this is not day and night as we calculate it due to the rotation of the earth, but this is the beginning of time as God calculates days and systems in his creation.

We live in a physical realm of **space, time, and matter**! In the **beginning was time, heaven was space and Earth was matter**. God set up the physical dimensions along with time as the framework for our existence.

Again, we see the contrasting **binary code** of creation in these three verses: **light and dark, day and night, and morning and evening**. And this is just the first day!

The 2nd Day- Atmosphere & Ocean

"Then God said, "Let there be a ***firmament*** in the midst of the ***waters***, and let it ***divide*** the waters from the waters. Thus, God made the firmament, and ***divided*** the waters which were under the firmament from the waters which were above the firmament; and it was so. And God called the firmament ***Heaven***. So, the evening and the morning were the second day." Genesis 1:6-8

Here we see on the ***second day,*** a **second division**. God separates the **atmospheric heaven** from the **waters on the earth**. Perhaps this firmament is the clouds that contain water. Some believe the atmosphere may have been some sort of watery dome above the earth because the scriptures talk about a mist watering the earth:

"And every plant of the field before it was in the earth, and every herb of the field before it grew: for the Lord God had not caused it to rain upon the earth, and there was not a man to till the ground. But there went up ***a mist*** from the earth and ***watered the whole face of the ground***." Genesis 2:5-6

The word **mist** could mean **vapor,** and some speculate that this is the water evaporation cycle. However, that is unlikely since it did not rain until the flood. A mist suggests a condensation and fine water droplets, but we are given the clue in Genesis 7:11:

"...all the fountains of the great deep burst open, and the ***floodgates of the sky were opened.***"

This confirms that the atmosphere was a watery firmament. And so, we see again a separation of the waters above from the waters below. God's **binary** code is utilized on the second day.

The 3rd Day- Land & Seas

"Then God said, 'Let the ***waters*** under the heavens be gathered together into one place, and let the ***dry land*** appear'; and it was so. And God called the dry land ***Earth***, and the gathering together of the waters He called ***Seas***. And God saw that it was good. Then God said, 'Let the earth bring forth ***grass***, the herb that yields ***seed***, and the ***fruit tree*** that yields fruit according to its kind, whose seed is in itself, on the earth'; and it was so. And the earth brought forth grass, the herb that yields seed according to its kind, and the tree that yields fruit, whose seed is in itself according to its kind. And God saw that it was good. So, the evening and the morning were the third day." Genesis 1:9-13

On the ***third day,*** God separates the **oceans** from the **land.** The seas would provide **water** which is essential for life. The oceans also produce 50 to 85 percent of oxygen for man through photosynthesizing algae and phytoplankton in sunlight. Man could not, however, live on the **wet ocean waters** so God brought forth **dry land** and separated it from the seas as the habitation for man.

From **seed, grass** (wheat, grains, etc.), and **fruit trees** he would produce **food** for man. Trees and vegetation also help produce **oxygen** for man to breathe! God also made a binary symbiotic system where plants give off oxygen to benefit man and man breathes out carbon dioxide to benefit plants!

The **earth** and **seas** are widely different from each other, but the combination of those distinctions made a perfect environment for man…so again we see on the third day of creation a two-fold work, a ***Binary Life system*** created for mankind.

The 4th Day- Planets, Sun, Moon, and Stars

"Then God said, 'Let there be ***lights in the firmament of the heavens*** to divide the ***day from the night***; and let them be for ***signs and seasons***, and for ***days and years***; and let them be for lights in the firmament of the heavens ***to give light on the earth***'; and it was so. Then God made ***two great lights***: the ***greater light*** to rule the day, and the ***lesser light*** to rule the night. He made the ***stars*** also. God set them in the firmament of the heavens ***to give light on the earth***, and to rule over the day and over the night, and **to divide the light from the darkness**. And God saw that it was good. So, the evening and the morning were the fourth day." Genesis 1:14-19

On the ***fourth day*** of creation, God creates the **planets, sun and moon, and stars**. This is what will give man measurable **time** for seasons and "days and years" as well as light. The **sun** is the **greater light** and gives us our **days** and the **moon** and stars are the **lesser light** which give us our **night**. So now we have the ***binary time system*** of Night and Day. This is the beginning of man's time frame, for we measure time in days, years, and seasons by the movement of the heavenly bodies as well as by the sun, moon, and earth. Yet, to God who measures time by the creation of binary systems and events, this is simply the **fourth day** of creation.

The 5th Day- Ocean Animals & Sky Animals

"Then God said, "Let the ***oceans swarm with living creatures***, and let ***flying creatures soar above the earth throughout the sky***!" So, God created every kind of magnificent ***marine creature***, every kind of living marine crawler with which the waters swarmed, and ***every kind of flying creature***. And God saw how good it was. God blessed them by saying, "Be fruitful, multiply, and ***fill the oceans***. Let the ***birds multiply*** throughout the earth!" The twilight and the dawn were the fifth day." Genesis 1:20-23 (ISV)

On the ***fifth day,*** God continues with his binary creation. Up to this point, he has created the containers, environment, and habitat for life, so now he starts to create **living creatures for the oceans** and the **flying birds for the sky**. Again, we see two distinct creations for two different environments: a **binary system** of **fish with gills** and **birds with wings-** completely different from each other, yet perfectly suited for their own environment. Why does God focus on a **duel pattern** each day? Because he is setting it up for man to see the work of **division, separation, and distinction**- to prepare him for the **dual nature of life.**

The 6th Day- Land Animals and Mankind

The ***sixth day*** is set up for the dual creation of animals and man. God made a beautiful, physical planet but it was barren of **a special creation of intellectual and spiritual qualities** to live in this incredible environment. Before He brings man on the scene, He must create the animal kingdom as companions (and later sacrifices and food). He has brought forth living creatures for the seas and the air and now He must make animals for the land.

"And God said, "Let the land produce living creatures according to their kinds: the livestock, the creatures that move along the ground, and the wild animals, each according to its kind." And it was so. God made the wild animals according to their kinds, the livestock according to their kinds, and all the creatures that move along the ground according to their kinds. And God saw that it was good." Genesis 1:24-25 (NIV)

Now the scene is set. God does not work randomly or haphazardly but has carefully prepared a binary world for this moment. He now begins the crown of his creation…man!

" Then God said, "Let us make ***mankind in our image***, in ***our likeness***, so that ***they may rule over the fish in the sea and the birds in the sky, over the livestock and all the wild animals, and over all the creatures that*** *move along the ground*." So God created mankind in his own image, in the image of God he created them; ***male and female*** he created them. God blessed them and said to them, "Be fruitful and increase in number; fill the earth and subdue it. ***Rule over the fish in the sea and the birds in the sky and over every living creature that moves on the ground***." Then God said, "I give you every ***seed-bearing plant*** on the face of the whole earth and every tree that ***has fruit with seed in it***. They will be yours for food. And to all the beasts of the earth and all the birds in the sky and ***all the creatures that move along the ground***—everything that has the breath of life in it—***I give every green plant for food***." And it was so. God saw all that he had made, and it was very good. And there was evening, and there was morning—the sixth day. " Genesis 1:26-31 (NIV)

On the ***sixth and last day* of Creation** He creates the **land animals** and **man**. The inhabitants of the land would be unique creations. God would name man Adam, and later Adam would name the animals. This is not low-level inferior cavemen with ancient Neanderthal intellect as we are taught by scientists. Nor is this indicative of a man evolving out of some prehistoric goo! Adam naming the animals shows communication and language and intellect as he was made in the image of God!

In the creation of animals and man we see that **God made them male and female. This is the *binary system of sexual gender*.** In today's modern culture where we have adopted multi-gender and transgender forms, we are defying the binary principles of the creation itself!

The 7th Day- Division of Work and Rest

"Thus the heavens and the earth were finished, and all the host of them. And on the seventh day ***God ended his work*** which he had made; and he ***rested on the seventh day from all his work*** which he had made. And God blessed the seventh day, and sanctified it: because that in it ***he had rested from all his work which God created and made***." Genesis 2:1-3

On the ***seventh day,*** we see God's Sabbath contrasting the **two principles** of **work** and **rest**. God did not rest because He was tired. He ceased His labor in order to **stop and enjoy it.** His creation gave him pleasure and He gave us the example of **rest** and **reflection**. This would show the importance of both **creation and recreation!**

God shows us not to just plant the roses and prune them, but to stop and smell them and view their beauty. One of the Ten Commandments is to honor the **Sabbath** and keep it holy. But Jesus said that man was not made for the Sabbath but the **Sabbath for man**.

God rested on the ***seventh day*** so He could reflect upon His work and see its beauty. Even at the end of each creation day He paused to say "**it was good**" so at the end of His creation week He **ceased His labor** in order to **enjoy the goodness of His works**. The Sabbath is for **rest and reflection and** He left this binary code as an example for us!

The Binary Companion

The end of chapter two of Genesis goes into further detail of the creation of Adam. Man was formed out of the land that he was put upon. The very dust of the earth became the building blocks of his physical body with all its intricacies, complexities and uniqueness. Man was different than all other creations. Our bodies are a complex creation of **multiple binary systems** such as **two arms and two legs, two eyes, two ears, two hands, two feet, two nostrils, two breasts.** Woman have **two ovaries** and men **two testicles** and inwardly we have many organs that come in pairs, such as the **lungs, kidneys, and adrenal glands**. Man also has **two sets of ribs** and it was by one of these that God would use the DNA to make woman!

First, it must be pointed out that Adam's body, as incredible as it was made, was dead until God breathed life into him. It is the **binary system** of the **body** and the **breath** that made Adam a living soul.

Now there is an important observation here! In all the things that God created He said afterwards "**it was good.**" God is good and made all things good and perfect. God walked with Adam in the cool of the day each day, but He realized that Man needed one of his own kind as a companion and helper. For the first time, God said "***It is not good***"!

"The LORD God said, 'It is ***not good*** ***for the man to be alone***. I will make a helper suitable for him.' Genesis 2:18 (NIV)

Interestingly, He did not immediately make Eve. Instead, He brought all the animals to Adam to name [Adam would also name Eve (Gen. 3:20)]. Perhaps he was allowing Adam to see that all the animals had a female companion, but Adam did not. Perhaps he was stirring upon Adam the realization that although he was unique, he was also in need of a similar companion of his own **kind**.

Adam had been made from the dust of the earth and God could have done the same with Eve, but instead He put Adam into a **deep sleep** and performed an operation to **take a part out of him** so that she would always **be a part of him**. God took bone to construct woman from man's DNA! Not only would she be a companion to him, but she would thus begin the cycle of reproduction that would allow people to inhabit the earth. Thus, Adam said:

"This is now ***bone of my bones*** and ***flesh of my flesh***; She shall be called ***Woman***, because she was ***taken out of Man***." Genesis 2:23

Now, man has become a binary species. Two genders, similar and, yet, quite different.

The Binary Trees of Eden

> "And out of the ground made the Lord God to grow every tree that is pleasant to the sight, and good for food; ***the tree of life*** also in the midst of the garden, and ***the tree of knowledge of good and evil***." Genesis 2:9

The Garden of Eden was a microcosm of the world. It was where food was provided by luscious fruit trees and work was enjoyable and fulfilling. It was also where a beautiful companion had now been provided to share the blessings with. Yet, as God did in the creation, He continued the binary principle of opposites in the Garden. He did so by placing two unique trees in Eden: The **Tree of the Knowledge of Good and Evil** and the **Tree of Life**. The contrast could not be greater, for one represented **eternal** life and the other **death**.

God had given man free will, but in order for man to truly be free he needed to be **free to choose**. So, a **two-fold binary decision** of choice was given to Adam:

> "And the Lord God commanded the man, saying, 'Of every tree of the garden you may freely eat; but of ***the tree of the knowledge of good and evil*** you shall not eat, for in the day that you eat of it **you shall surely *die*.**'" Genesis 2:16,17 (NKJV)

The binary principle often requires **separation or division.** Death here was **spiritual death** which ultimately leads to **physical death.** One separates the **spirit of man from God**. The other separates **the soul of man from the body.**

Now God never forbade Adam and Eve not to eat of the Tree of Life. They could have had eternal life had they done so. It was only necessary to put one tree in the garden and set parameters that would require either **obedience** or **disobedience.** This moral binary code would either lead to righteousness or sin.

Up until now, we have seen in creation the opposing forces of **heaven and earth, light and dark**, **day and night**, and **work and rest.** Now, through the two trees and the two choices, we see in the garden of Eden the binary principle of **good and bad, obedience and disobedience, and life** and **death!**

Obedience vs Disobedience

In the next chapter, we will see how the Tempter made his way into the garden. However, it is important to know that though God made a perfect world, it could not be perfect if men were robots or slaves or were void of free will and choice. God, being good, had to allow man the option to choose right from wrong! God was not worried however, because even before the earth was made, He made a backup plan (which we will see later).

The serpent (Satan) **separated** Eve from Adam and began to **question** God's truthfulness to her in order to bring **doubt** and disbelief rather than **faith.** It would challenge them both to either o**bey** God or **disobey** Him!

> "Now the ***serpent*** was more subtle than any beast of the field which the LORD God had made. And he said unto the woman, 'Yea, ***hath God said***, Ye shall not eat of every tree of the garden?' And the woman said unto the serpent, 'We may eat of the fruit of the trees of the garden: But of the fruit of the tree which is in the midst of the garden, God hath said, 'Ye shall not eat of it, neither shall ye touch it, lest ye die'. And the serpent said unto the woman, ***'Ye shall not surely die:*** For God doth know that in the day ye eat thereof, then your eyes shall be opened, and ***ye shall be as gods***, ***knowing good and evil***'. And when the woman saw that the tree was good for food, and that it was pleasant to the eyes, and a tree to be desired to make one wise, she took of the fruit thereof, and did eat, and gave also unto her husband with her; and he did eat. And the eyes of them both were opened... and they knew that they were naked." Genesis 3:1-7

Satan challenges the **Creator** by telling Eve she can eat any tree in the Garden. Eve responds by saying that no, they were not to eat from the tree in the middle of the garden (The Tree of the knowledge of **Good** and **Evil**) or they would die. The bible says that Satan is a liar and the Father of Lies (John 8:44). He blatantly lies to Eve and says, "***You shall not Die!***" but rather "your **eyes will be opened"** and they would **"be like God's"**.

Satan always tells **half-truths** to sneak in the **lie**. That is why he is so **subtle**. Adam and Eve would not die **immediately,** but they would now put an expiration date on their bodies and would eventually physically die. They chose to disobey God and, in essence, they were poisoned by that fruit. Their DNA was altered and now entropy would begin, and their bodies would slowly age and die! He told the truth about their "**eyes being opened,"** but that was not necessarily a good thing. The tree was called the

Tree of the Knowledge of **Good** and **Evil** because now an **understanding of evil** would be brought to man's awareness.

Now their eyes were opened, and they would see that they were naked and exposed! When God came to Adam and Eve in the cool of the day, they **hid from him**. Now instead of **faith** they possessed **fear**. How did a perfect world become so **imperfect**? Many ask why God brought evil into the world, but He did not. He simply allowed man to make one of two choices: **truth or error, obedience or disobedience, good or evil, life or death.** This is the **binary code of choice**: two opposing forces that man can choose.

God did not create **darkness**. He allowed it to exist but brought forth light to compound it. He did not bring **evil** into the Garden, He allowed it to come in, to test man's loyalty and faith. He did not cause them to fall- He gave them the choice to obey or disobey. So, where did all this **darkness and evil** come from? It started in **the war in heaven!**

Design and Chance

Up to now we have seen the biblical account of God's creation! There is however now presently a binary challenge to the work of creation! Until recent times, nearly all tribes and nations believed in God. Some believed in a single God and some in many Gods. Some worshiped idols as God- but the universal belief in a deity has occurred in every generation of history until the 19th century! This so-called A**ge of Reason** began to shed biblical thinking and elevate humanistic science above scriptures.

Though some naturalists prior to Darwin propose various evolutionary ideas, it was Charles Darwin who popularized the idea through his writings. Initially, this was called the "Theory" of Evolution, but today nearly every scientist thinks it is fact. Evolution is taught in all school levels today so that by the time one gets out of college he has been thoroughly indoctrinated into this fallacy! Evolution perfectly fits into the bible's description of the end times:

> "Now the Spirit speaketh expressly, that in the latter times some shall ***depart from the faith***, giving heed to seducing spirits, and ***doctrines of devils***." 1 Timothy 4:1

Doctrine simply means teaching and Timothy prophesied that in the end times some kind of new teaching would lead many astray. Evolution is the greatest threat to biblical creationism because it not only defiantly declares that God did not make man, but it promotes Atheism by declaring that through evolutionary processes there is no need for God!

The foolishness of evolution is not only contrary to God's word, but even opposes the second Laws of Thermodynamics which state that things fall apart over time and decay rather than improve and get better. We use to once believe in **"observable science"** and that it coincided with biblical principles. But science went from observable and repeatable to **theoretical**! Science used to be based on facts that were **observable, measurable and repeatable**. Science has now moved into a purely theoretical concept. Physics, such as particle theory, is now theoretical because it is no longer based on observation but on opinions and speculation. Astronomy is no longer based on what we observe through telescopes and the naked eye, but rather on theoretical speculation of what is unseen. Astronomers now theorize on what they assume happened in the past, not what they presently observe. The Big Bang theory is a good example. We cannot observe it, have no witnesses to it, have no proof it ever happened, but it is now taken as fact. The apostle Paul said:

> "O Timothy, keep that which is committed to thy trust, avoiding profane and vain babblings, and oppositions of ***science falsely so called,*** Which some professing have erred concerning the faith."
> 1 Timothy 6:20

He is saying that there is a **so-called science** that causes many to error! Biology has removed the Creator from the creation so that now there is no sanctity for life or biological marriage! Abortion is the norm. Infanticide, assistant suicide, same-sex marriage, pedophilia and transgender are becoming the norm. This is why Paul referred it to "doctrines of demons". These are not just human teachings, but demonic and satanic in origin.

The foolishness of life coming from chance and simplicity begetting complexity, or the vastness of such a highly developed and beautiful world can only be explained as being from the hand of a divine designer, not a long-term slow process of haphazard random accidents. The Law of Entropy states that things over time get worse, not better!You stick a car in a yard and after a while, it rusts and falls apart. You leave a building over centuries and it decays and falls into ruin.Yet so-called wise men of science want us to believe that not only will things evolve upward over time but that complexity will come forth without God if we just give it enough time!

> *"Professing themselves to be wise, they became fools." Romans 1:22*

The only witness to Creation was the Trinity of God and the Angels. God has testified to his creation by dictating Genesis (and the first five books of the Bible) to Moses so that man would know where he truly came from. But now the modern progressive man says like the devil "Hath God said?" When Satan questioned God he lied knowingly. Today's so called scientist lie by denouncing the bible as myth and even call into question the very existence of our loving Creator. Men who oppose God will suffer the same fate as the angels and Satan when they try to oppose God. In the next chapter we will learn of the division of the angels and the Binary war that occurred in heaven!

Chapter 2 - The Two Armies - the Binary Code in Heaven

Lucifer the Light Bearer

The story of Lucifer's fall is described in two key Old Testament chapters: Ezekiel 28 and Isaiah 14.

Evil came into being either before or right after the earth was made! It started with a high-ranking angel named Lucifer. Angels too were created beings perfect in all their ways until sin was found in Lucifer's heart through pride. He started a war in heaven and lost and then Lucifer (Satan) and the demons were banished from heaven and kicked out and fell to the earth. This is who entered the Garden of Eden as evil and revengeful towards God; this is who sought to persuade the first couple to rebel and be disobedient against God.

> "***Thou hast been in Eden the garden*** of God; every ***precious stone*** was thy covering, the sardius, topaz, and the diamond, the beryl, the onyx, and the jasper, the sapphire, the emerald, and the carbuncle, and gold: the workmanship of thy tabrets and of thy pipes was prepared in thee in the day that thou wast created. Thou art the ***anointed cherub*** that covereth; and I have set thee so: thou wast upon ***the holy mountain of God***; thou hast walked up and down in the midst of the stones of fire. Thou wast ***perfect*** in thy ways from the day that thou wast created, ***till iniquity was found in thee.***" Ezekiel 28:13-15

Lucifer was once glorious. His name means "shining one", "morning star" or "light bearer". This is perhaps because of the beauty of his adornment in precious stones or in his anointing as he is called the anointed cherub. But **pride** crept in his heart and began to change his nature.

> "Thine heart was lifted up ***because of thy beauty***, thou hast corrupted thy wisdom by reason of thy brightness" Ezekiel 28:17

We now see the beginning of the first binary nature of sin. A **division** suddenly occurred in the ranks of the angels. One of God's highest ark angel started to get puffed up and turned praise from **God** to **himself**. This angel of praise changed pronouns from **you** to **I**. He went from **perfection** to **corruption**. God gave him his beauty, but he became corrupted by that beauty and turned against his Maker. He turned from being the **angel of light** to the **prince of darkness!**

He was not content to be a servant of God, he wanted to **be God**. Now his evil passion was **power**! He wanted the very throne of God himself and thus caused a war of rebellion in Heaven. Instead of obtaining God's throne however, he and a third of the angels (Rev. 12:14) were now banished and kicked out of heaven. Satan had sought to change things in Heaven but only brought about horrible changes to himself and his followers:

> "I will ***cast thee to the ground,*** I will lay thee before kings, that they may behold thee. Thou hast ***defiled*** thy sanctuaries by the multitude of thine ***iniquities***, by the iniquity of thy traffic; therefore will I bring forth ***a fire from the midst of thee, it shall devour thee, and I will bring thee to ashes upon the earth in the sight of all them that behold thee.*** All they that know thee among the people shall be astonished at thee: thou shalt be a terror, and never shalt thou be any more." Ezekiel 28:17-19

Change in Nature

Satan's nature had completely changed, and his character became perverted. As it says above: a "**fire within him**" began to "**devour him.**" Iniquity or **sin** was found in him as pride took over. He had become **corrupt** and **self-serving**. He had become unholy, ungrateful and filled with hatred for God. Lucifer went from a beautiful highly adorned angel to a dark and hideous creature.

Although the bible says he can sometime masquerade as an angel of light (2 Cor. 11:14) Satan was no longer one. He was once **pure** but now **defiled**; **holy** but now **unholy**; **submissive** but now **self-serving**; **humble** but now **proud**; ambitiously seeking **power!** Lucifer had now become **corrupted** by his own pride and now sought to corrupt others. He led a war in heaven between loyal angels and deceived angels, but they would eventually lose and be kicked out of heaven.

The **rebellious** fallen angels now would have their nature changed as well. They would become demons and devils possessing the same **evil** nature as the one they chose to follow! The binary laws began, **good** vs **evil**, **obedience** vs **disobedience**, **war** vs **peace**.

Change in Position

"How art thou *fallen* from *heaven*, O Lucifer, son of the morning! How art thou *cut down to the ground*, which didst weaken the nations! For thou hast said in thine heart, ***I will ascend into heaven, I will exalt my throne above the stars of God: I will sit also upon the mount of the congregation, in the sides of the north: I will ascend above the heights of the clouds; I will be like the most High. Yet thou shalt be brought down to hell, to the sides of the pit.***" Isaiah 14:12-15

Satan had sought the very throne of God. He wanted sole authority over all the angels. He sought to be **above,** and he ended up **below**. The binary positions of polar opposites would now encompass his position. He wanted to be God but became God's greatest adversary. He sought the highest **heaven** but was brought down to **hell**. Even Jesus spoke of the Fall of Satan which proves the Lord's pre-existence in the beginning!

"And he said unto them, I beheld ***Satan*** as lightning ***fall*** from heaven!" Luke 10:18

God could not allow Satan and his followers to continue to stay in heaven lest they corrupt others. He and his cohorts were banished! They fell to earth. Some believe that God put hell into the center of the earth and perhaps this is why they fell to earth. We know that some fallen angels have been imprison there until the end-times (1 Peter 3:18-20, Jude 1:6, Rev. 9:1-12) and many are kept in hell until judgment (1Peter 2:4).

Hell is simply a prison until final sentencing comes. In Revelation, we see the final destination is the eternal Lake of Fire. Tragic how Satan's position will eternally change from being by the side of a good and gracious God to being isolated in a burning, fiery lake, forever!

Change in Name

"Then ***war*** broke out in heaven. Michael and his angels fought against the dragon, and the dragon and his angels fought back. But he was not strong enough, and they lost their place in heaven. The great dragon was hurled down—that ancient serpent called the devil, or ***Satan***, who leads the whole world astray. He was hurled to the earth, and his angels with him." Revelation 12:7–10 (NIV)

Lucifer, the light bearer's name, was changed to **Satan** (nicknamed the devil or the serpent or dragon) after the fall.

Satan means **"adversary"** or "one who **resists"** or "the **accuser."** He once had God's great favor, but now he became God's great adversary. The binary code now reveals the duel opposing forces of good and evil. Nearly every novel has the same plot. A protagonist and an antagonist. The protagonist is the hero- the good guy in white- and the protagonist is the bad guy in black. Satan caused division and still does. He still opposes God. Rather than repenting, feeling remorseful and learning his lesson, Satan chooses to continue the battle on earth using man in his fallen state.

Satan means "one who resists" or "an opposer." He is consumed by hate and seeks to destroy God, his people and His plan. He sought to thwart the plan of salvation by crucifying God's son, but he only succeeded in bring about the redemption of man! The Bible calls Satan "the **accuser** of the brethren" and "the father of lies." Jesus said he was a liar from the beginning. No doubt he lied to other angels, deceiving them into thinking God was their enemy (as he has done the same to man.) **He deceived them into thinking he could defeat God;** no doubt they probably regret following him now. Adversary means enemy. Lucifer was a trusted friend of God and now he has become his arch enemy. He is also the adversary of man:

> "Be sober, be vigilant; because ***your adversary*** the devil, as a roaring lion, walks about, ***seeking whom he may devour***" 1 Peter 5:8

The I Will and the I Am

Five times Satan declared "I will", in defiance to God!

> "How art thou fallen from heaven, O Lucifer, son of the morning! How art thou cut down to the ground, which didst weaken the nations! For thou hast said in thine heart,
> ***I will*** ascend into heaven,
> ***I will*** exalt my throne above the stars of God:
> ***I will*** sit also upon the mount of the congregation,
> in the sides of the north:
> ***I will*** ascend above the heights of the clouds;
> ***I will*** be like the most High.
> Yet thou shalt be brought down to hell, to the sides of the pit." Isaiah 14:12-15

His arrogant declaration and self-elevation of equality with God was probably his campaign promises to the third of the angels that he got to revolt in Heaven. However, his desire for ascension brought him down. His ego's desire for elevation got him kicked out and his desire to be like God made him nothing like God but the very opposite of God. Now a **binary war** brought not only a **division of heaven** but **two opposing forces**. God is Light and Satan is the prince of Darkness. God is Love and Satan is the epitome of hate. God is the giver of Life and Satan comes to "steal, kill and destroy!" Jesus brought forth Life and Satan brought forth Death. **Satan's evil ambition declared five" I will"s. But Jesus would combat it with seven "I am"s.**

Jesus declared to be the "I am":

- I am the Bread of Life (John 6:35)
- I am the Light of the world (John 8:12, 9:5)
- I am the Door of the sheep (John 10:7)
- I am the Resurrection and the Life (John 11:25)
- I am the Way and the Truth and the Life (John 14:6)
- I am the true Vine (John 15:1)
- I am the Alpha and the Omega (Rev. 1:8)

Jesus's seven "**I Am's**" are **greater** than Lucifer's five "**I Will's**!" An "**I will**" speaks of an attempt at an **action**. Satan **failed** in all those actions. He accomplished none of them. This is the reason he is called the "father of lies". His five declarations were the **first lies ever uttered!** Jesus told the Pharisees who were being led by the devil:

> "You belong to your father, ***the devil***, and you want to carry out your father's desires. He was a murderer from the beginning, ***not holding to the truth***, for there is ***no truth in him. When he lies, he speaks his native language***, for ***he is a liar and the father of lies***." John 8:44 (NIV)

Jesus declared seven times "I am!" An "**I am**" is a personal characteristic. It is a declaration of who someone is as well as their intrinsic nature. Jesus speaks the truth because he is all that he declared himself to be! Personal **character** triumphs over empty **aspirations**!

There is much confusion about the **equality** of Satan and God. Though they are opposites in function, they are in no way the same in being. **Satan and God are not equa**l. God is **far greater** than Satan. Satan is a created being and God is his creator! Satan is an adversary of God and an opposer of God, but Satan is in no way equal to the power, majesty and greatness of

God. Though he lured a third of the angels to rebellion and perhaps more so of men, he did not keep his first estate and was kicked out of heaven; and all his followers will make their final destiny in the Lake of fire.

> "And ***the angels which kept not their first estate, but left their own habitation***, he hath reserved in everlasting chains under darkness unto the ***judgment*** of the great day." Jude 1:6

To show you how powerless Satan is, God has shown him his destiny and Satan can do nothing to avert it. All Satan had to do was stop one of God's prophecies from happening or thwart the plans of God, but Satan does not have the power to do so because God is now the beginning and the end. God sees outside the realm of time and knows what will happen before it happens and Satan does not have the ability to alter what was, what is or what will be. Jesus, however, is "He who was, and is, and is to come (Rev. 8:1).

The same is true of the Son of God and the Antichrist. Although the Antichrist and the true Christ are opposites, they are not equal. Jesus is far more supreme than the worst dictator in history, as the ruler of the universe is much greater than the ruler of the world! Again, the antichrist is a created being and Jesus is the Creator (Col. 1:16).

The Antichrist is a counterfeit Christ. He may claim to do supernatural events that look like miracles, but he is all about deception. He may recover from a head wound and mimic a resurrection, but he is nothing like the true Messiah that conquered death, hell and the grave and ascended to the right hand of God!

The **binary armies** not only clashed in heaven, but they will clash on earth. Jesus and the redeemed, along with his angels, will war with the Antichrist and wicked men on earth, yet the heavenly army will easily defeat the earthly army. They will be destroyed by the very brightness of his coming and one single angel will throw Satan into the Lake of Fire. Then the words of Isaiah will ring true:

> "Those who see you stare at you, they ponder your fate: '***Is this the man*** who shook the earth and made kingdoms tremble, the man who made the world a wilderness, who overthrew its cities and would not let his captives go home?' All the kings of the nations lie in each in his own tomb. But you are cast out of your tomb..." Isaiah14:16-19 (NIV)

> "You are brought down to hell" Isaiah 14:15

Chapter 3 - The Two Choices – the Binary Code of Free Will

God's Side or the Devil's Side

God allowed the angels to choose to align themselves with **Lucifer** or **Himself**. But he also made **consequences** for that decision. He did the same for Adam and Eve, allowing them to choose to **obey** or **disobey** and telling them the **consequence of disobedience**. He gave them **a wide berth in allowances** to fully enjoy all his creations, All the beauty and pleasures of the garden, the provision of luscious fruit and enjoyment of the animals were all at their disposal, but with that wide birth of privileges and allowances he also gave them **a very small sliver of restriction** to test their loyalty and permit them the freedom to choose for themselves. Yet God also knew how they would respond even though he told them that if they disobeyed and ate of the Tree of the Knowledge of Good and Evil, they would set in motion the **spirit of death**. Afterwards, he also **banned** them from the garden as he banned Satan and the demons from heaven. He put an angel with a flaming sword to guard the **Tree of Life** lest they eat it and be eternally lost without redemption.

He then pronounced a **curse** upon them for their disobedience. This would be the natural ramification for yielding to temptation and disobeying God's only rule! They both would have pain in labor! Eve would have pain in labor in giving birth and Adam would have pain in physical labor by having to work by the sweat of his brow due to a cursed ground from which he came.

Ultimately, all mankind will have to choose a side just as the angels did. We all must choose to be on either **Gods side** or the **Devil's side**. There are no other **choices**. Only two! This is the **binary code of choice**. Man may not willfully choose to follow or even believe in the Devil, but it doesn't matter. ***No choice is a choice by default***. Jesus said:

> "He who is not with Me is against Me, and he who does not gather with Me scatters." Matthew 12:30

When sin entered the first couple, it **corrupted their DNA,** and that

corruption would now be passed on to their children and ultimately to all mankind. Paul said:

> "Wherefore, as by ***one man sin entered into the world, and death*** by sin; and ***so death passed upon all men***, for that all have sinned." Romans 5:12

Sin now has become a **genetic defect**. It and the consequence of sin and death is now inherited by all men. The garden was about the **binary choice of Life or Death** and man chose death. However, God knew beforehand what Adam would do and as he prepared a body in Adam that led to sin through disobedience, he also prepared a body before the foundations of the earth which would lead to redemption only through obedience. This would come later.

Sin and that one act of disobedience would change man as it changed Lucifer. When God came into the garden after the fall for the first time, **Adam and his wife hid from God.** For the very first time, they felt the power of **FEAR**!

Binary Force of Fear vs Faith.

Fear is a terrible force. It is a force that only works on oneself. Fear simply torments the person who is under it. The bible says:

> "There is no fear in love; but perfect love casteth out fear: because ***fear hath torment.*** He that feareth is not made perfect in love." John 4:18

Fear is tormenting. It is painful and emotionally paralyzing and fear can lead to madness and death.

I have never understood man's fascination with horror movies and shows that make you afraid! I never much liked horror films, but many with the nature of sin seem to gravitate to it even now. As a teenager, I did marijuana, LSD and other drugs which was very common in the late sixties and seventies. I noticed that though sometime the euphoria and visual aspects were quite interesting, they came with what was commonly referred to as "**paranoia.**" This is nothing but another form of fear and certainly can be tormenting!

The Greek word here for **torment** can actually be translated a different way. Another version puts it this way:

> "There is no fear in love; but perfect love casts out fear, because ***fear involves punishment***, and the one who fears is not perfected in love." 1 John 4:18 (NAS)

Adam and Eve hid for **fear of punishment**. If a child does something wrong, he is afraid that he is going to get punished so he tries to hide his sin from his parents. We often do the same. The bible says that when Jesus comes back to judge the wicked that men will hide in caves for fear of God's wrath and punishment.

> "Then the kings of the earth, the princes, the generals, the rich, the mighty, and everyone else, both slave and free, ***hid in caves and among the rocks of the mountains***. They called to the mountains and the rocks, 'Fall on us and ***hide*** us from the face of him who sits on the throne and from the wrath of the Lamb!'" Revelation 6:15-16 (NIV)

These men whose conscience had been seared like a hot iron were impervious to God when they thought he was far away and not watching, yet the minute they realized he returned they were suddenly gripped with fear for they realize the punishment is about to be doled out! Even Satan knows his time is getting short so he is getting more afraid because the final punishment will be the Lake of Fire!

> " And the great dragon was cast out, that old serpent, called the Devil, and Satan, which deceiveth the whole world: he was cast out into the earth, and his angels were cast out with him. Therefore rejoice, ye heavens, and ye that dwell in them. Woe to the inhabiters of the earth and of the sea! for the devil is come down unto you, having great wrath, because he knoweth that he hath but a short time." Revelation 12:9, 12

We will see later more on the binary code of **punishment** and **reward**. God **rewards** us for obedience but there is **punishment** for disobedience! There is a judgment seat of God whereby all will be judged for their deeds and all will either be **rewarded** or **punished**.

Binary Force of Love and Hate

The Bible says God is **Love** (1 John 4:8) but sin has the opposing force of **Hate**. Love **gives**, hate **takes**. Satan, because of his own pride and selfishness began to hate God and wanted to depose Him and take away his throne. He desired to take as **many angels** from him as he could, and now, he wants to take **as many men into hell as he can.** He is utterly selfish and is consumed with hate! Hatred leads to every evil work.

> "Hatred stirs up strife, but love covers all offenses." Proverbs 10:12. (ESV)

Hatred provokes division and strife which cause fighting and wars. Hate blinds men to the truth and often divides them. Hate judges others by color or class and stirs up political divide, and hate can ultimately lead to murder.

The very first generation of Adam and Eve produced two children: **Cain and Abel**. Cain was jealous of his brother Abel and hated him because Abel properly offered a **blood sacrifice** of an innocent animal as a covering for his sins. Abel knew of the pattern that when Adam and Eve sinned God covered them in animal skins. Those **animals shed their blood as a symbol of Christ** who was to come to shed his blood for mankind. Later in the tabernacle and temple, this practice would be carried on as **a prototype and prophetic act that would point to Christ**.

Cain, however, offered the work of his own hands, the fruit of the **cursed ground,** but the bible says:

> "Indeed, under the law almost everything is ***purified with blood***, and ***without the shedding of blood there is no forgiveness of sins***." Hebrews 9:22 (RSV)

This force of Hate had its roots in jealousy just as Satan initially was jealous of God. But jealousy has a progression! Cain's **jealousy** led to **anger**, then to **hate** and finally to **murder**! Cain slew his brother and then tried to cover it up. But God said his **blood** cried up from the cursed ground. Cain, like Satan, allowed his selfish nature to take over. When God asked Cain where his brother was, Cain replied "Am I my brother's keeper" (Gen.4:9)

This pattern of jealousy, hatred and murder is all throughout the Bible! Hatred ultimate seeks to destroy!

- Esau was angry at his brother for stealing his birthright and his hatred initially drove him to seek to kill his brother.
- The brothers of Joseph were jealous of him and threw him in a pit and wanted to kill him but sold him instead.
- King Saul was envious of David and started hating him, leading him to seek David's life! Saul literally threw spears at him and constantly pursued him to take his life.
- Korah was jealous of Moses and led a rebellion like Lucifer did. Ultimately, the ground opened up and swallowed him and his followers and brought them straight down to hell.
- Haman sought to kill Mordecai and all the Jews because of hatred!
- The Pharisees were jealous of Jesus and hated him and sought to have him crucified.

There are many other examples, but the pattern is the same in a sinful heart. Whereas God is the source of **Love**, Satan is the source of **Hate**!

"But if you harbor bitter ***envy*** and ***selfish ambition*** in your hearts, do not boast about it or deny the truth. Such "wisdom" does not come down from heaven but is earthly, unspiritual, ***demonic***." James 3:14-15 (NIV)

We have been given the freedom to choose. We decide how we live, who we serve and how we conduct ourselves. **God warned Cain** even **after** slaying his brother that he had the choice to do good or bad, to make the proper choice or the wrong choice. That his free will gave him the ability to choose rightly or wrongly! We must rule over our sin nature and not allow it to rule over us!

"If you do ***what is right,*** will you not be accepted? But if you ***do not do what is right, sin*** is crouching at your door; it desires to have you, but ***you must rule over it***." Genesis 4:7 (NIV)

By following hate, we are being led by the same spirit that caused Lucifer to fall. By serving sin, we serve its source, Satan. We must master our heart and choose wisely. As Joshua said:

"...as for me and my house, we will serve the LORD." Joshua 24:15

Chapter 4 - The Two Paths - the Binary Code of Direction

There are actually only **two** directions. On a plane or globe there is North, South, East and West. But these can be broken into either **horizontal** or **vertical** directions! These can also be broken down into **two** directions. Vertical is either **up** or **down,** and horizontal is either **left** or **right**!

In 3D modeling or a in a 3D world, animators build everything using a 3-dimensional axis. They represent direction using 3 lines: X, Y or Z, which represent width, height and depth. However, these three directions are really broken down into **two binary directions** each, **up and down, left or right**, and **forward and backward.**

Not only does this represent our position and direction in physical space, but it also can represent our spiritual position and direction!

Left or Right Side

The Y axis or Horizontal axis represents width or the directions or position of right and left.

Everyone is either **left-handed** or **right-handed**. We have a **dominant hand** that initiates and leads and the other follows and helps. One is not necessarily better than the other, but certainly far more people are right-handed than left. According to Wikipedia, it is estimated that about 90% of people are right-handed and about 10% are left-handed! There are people who are **ambidextrous** and can use either hand; however, even **they have a preference of dominance!**

Interestingly, the Bible says that in the city of Nineveh there were more than 120,00 people who did not know their right hand from their left (Jonah 4:11). Some believe that these perhaps are children who did not understand left or right yet or perhaps some who were not smart enough. Perhaps this might indicate multiple ambidextrous people which would be extremely rare! More than likely, it symbolizes **not knowing the difference between wrong and right.** Yet they repented and God spared the city of judgment.

Right and left certainly are symbolic of right and wrong:

"A ***wise*** man's heart inclines him to the ***right***, but a ***fool's*** heart to the ***left***." Ecclesiastes 10:2 (ESV)

Right is symbolic of wisdom and left foolishness. Jesus implied this fact in the book of Matthew when he talks about the judgment in the end-times:

"When the Son of Man comes in his glory, and all the angels with him, he will sit on his glorious throne. All the nations will be gathered before him, and he will ***separate*** the people one from another as a shepherd separates the ***sheep*** from the ***goats***. He will put the ***sheep on his right*** and the ***goats on his left***." Matthew.25:31-33 (NIV)

The highest place of Honor is at the right side of God! After the resurrection of Jesus, he sat down at **the right hand of God** (Mark 16:19, Acts 7:55–56; Rom. 8:34; Eph. 1:20; Col. 3:1; Heb. 1:3; Heb. 8:1; Heb. 10:12; Heb. 12:2; 1 Peter 3:22; Rev. 3:21)

Interestingly, there were also **two thieves** on **both sides** of the cross next to Jesus.

"And with him they crucify two thieves; the one on ***his right hand,*** and the other on his ***left***." Mark 15:27

One was repentant and **one was not**. Although it did not say who was on each side, following this pattern it could very well be that the repented thief was on the right hand of Jesus and the unrepentant on the left! According to tradition, the Good Thief was crucified to Jesus's right and the other thief was crucified to his left. For this reason, depictions of the crucifixion of Jesus often show Jesus's head inclined to his right, showing his acceptance of the Good Thief.

"And one of the malefactors which were hanged railed on him, saying,' If thou be Christ, save thyself and us'. But the other answering rebuked him, saying, Dost not thou fear God, seeing thou art in the same condemnation? And ***we indeed justly; for we receive the due reward of our deeds:*** but this man hath done nothing amiss. And he said unto Jesus, Lord, remember me when thou comest into thy kingdom. And Jesus said unto him, Verily I say unto thee, ***today shalt thou be with me in paradise***." Luke 23:39-43

These two positions speak spiritually of all mankind. We will ***"...receive the due rewards of our deed!"*** but those who repent will find their eternal abode with Christ! We will all be either on one side of accepting him as Savior or the other side of rejecting him in our sins.

Two Gates and Two Roads

Jesus spoke of **two gates** and **two paths**. The two gates speak of the entry point to either the Kingdom of God or the gate that leads to the path of destruction.

> "Enter through ***the narrow gate***. For ***wide is the gate*** and ***broad is the road*** that leads to destruction, and many enter through it. But ***small is the gate*** and ***narrow the road*** that leads to life, and only a few find it." Matthew 7:13-14 (NIV)

As stated before, often **a binary system is a division or separation or two things that often oppose or contrast each other.** Jesus not only points the two paths we can travel on but shows the huge **differences** between the two. The gate is **wide,** and the road is **broad** that leads to destruction and **many** travel on it. It is the highway of the **many**, the freeway of the **multitude** and, dare I say sadly, the road of the **majority**! He contrasts that with the kingdom of God that has a **small** gate and a **narrow** path that **few** travel on. The **highway to hell** is abundant and populated with disbelieving or ignorant souls who have been led astray by the deceiver. The narrow **path of righteousness** is traveled by the **few** who believe and are faithful. Those who follow the majority are following each other to destruction, but those who break with the ranks and follow Christ will arise into eternal life!

Multitudes were killed in **the flood** and only **eight souls** from Noah's family were saved. The whole cities of **Sodom and Gomorrah** were wiped out but only **Lot and two daughters** escaped. The whole city of **Jericho** was destroyed but a believing harlot named **Rahab and her family** were the only survivors. The principle is clear. Do we go to the left or to the right when we come to the fork in the road? Do we choose the easiest road or the road most difficult? Do not make the false assumption that the majority rules or the majority is always right. God doesn't care about numbers. He leaves **the hundred** to go after **the one** who goes astray! God himself is the majority so the wise should align themselves with Him rather than follow the multitude that seek to oppose him! Pardon the pun, but you can either get on the **right** road or be **left** behind!

Forward or Backwards

After left and right, the second form of direction in a 3d axis is the X axis and represents Forward and backward! **forward** or **backwards** motion which is referred to as **depth**. This forward motion speaks of **spiritual depth** or **shallowness** of faith, being very committed or not very committed. We can have a very **deep** relationship with God or a very **superficial** one.

We normally **walk forward, or we walk backward,** and we can **move towards or away** from something.

Someone once said everybody is either moving towards God or moving away from God! God's desire is to bring us closer, but this starts with us drawing closer to him.

> "*Draw near to God* and He will *draw near to you!* Cleanse your hands, you sinners; and purify your hearts, you double-minded." James 4:8

God desires for us to draw near to him. Isaiah said:

> "*Seek* the LORD while He may be found; *Call* upon Him *while He is near*. Let the wicked forsake his way and the unrighteous man his thoughts; And let him return to the LORD, And He will have compassion on him, And to our God, For He will abundantly pardon." Isaiah 55:6-7 (NKJV)

The story of life is simply a story of man **falling away** and God calling him back. Jesus told the story of the prodigal son who leaves the father, then spends his inheritance and ends up empty and destitute. He had moved **backwards** and lost everything, but he got up and **moved forward** again returning to the father seeking forgiveness and the Father was standing at the door waiting for his return!

Sin has kept people from moving closer to God. It has separated man from his Creator. This was the purpose of Jesus's death and resurrection, so that he could reconcile us with God. The old testament allowed sin to be covered by the sacrifice of animals, but Jesus became the one sacrifice to allow us into God's presence through his blood.

> "But your *iniquities* have made a *separation* between you and your God, and your sins have hidden His face from you so that He does not hear." Isaiah 59:2 (ESV)

Now, unlike Adam who coward in fear in the presence of God, we can come closer to him boldly and in confidence when our sins are forgiven in Christ.

"Let us therefore ***come boldly*** unto the throne of grace, that we may obtain mercy, and find grace to help in time of need." Hebrews 4:16

Sadly, while many are finding salvation or growing in the Lord, others are departing from the faith. Some move **forward** and others move **backwards**. This is called **back**sliding.

"My people are bent on ***backsliding*** from Me. Though they call to the Most High, None at all exalt Him." Hosea 11:7(NKJV)

Many turn **back** instead of **forward**. Many return to the world and the old ways and sadly in the end-times, many will **depart from the faith**. The world has become more ungodly, more atheistic and soon will be governed by an anti-Christ spirit. Paul warned about this end-time falling away.

"Let no man deceive you by any means: for that day shall not come, except there come ***a falling away first,*** and that man of sin be revealed, the son of perdition" 2 Thessalonians 2:3

We cannot stay stationary in life. We must move **towards God** and **away from the world**. We must be a body in motion that seeks our Creator and returns to the original purpose of fellowship with God!

In some respect, we are **all moving forward** to destiny. **Time only moves forward for man** and we are all moving forward to the end-times, the return of Christ and judgment.

Up and Down

The last direction in a 3d axis is called the Z axis and represents the direction of up and down! It says in Psalms concerning forgiveness:

"For as ***high*** as the heavens are above the earth, so great is His loving devotion for those who fear Him. As ***far as the east is from the west***, so far has He removed our transgressions from us. As a father has compassion on his children, so the LORD has compassion on those who fear Him...." Psalm 103:11-12 (NIV)

The scriptures say our sins are removed from us as far as the east and the west. If you travel either east or west on the globe, you will go on for eternity. There is no end. Head east and you will always go east. Head west and you always go west. Not so with North and South! If you go north on the planet, once you get to the top you start heading south. If you head south, once you get to the bottom you start heading north. So East and West represent eternity or the infinite, whereas the directions North and South are finite. You can go **up to the highest heaven** or **down to the lowest hell,** but not beyond that!

The bible always speaks of **hell being down** and **heaven being up**. This will be the ultimate destination for all mankind. One place or the other, when Jesus comes back, he will rapture or resurrect his people and take them **up to heaven**. When the wicked die, they will **descend downward into hell**. This is the ultimate binary destinations for man and angels! We will talk more about that later.

Up also speaks to **being with God and in his presence.** When John was on the Isle of Patmos, he heard a word that told him "*Come **up** hither*". God called him **up** to heaven to see the visions of the end-times and told him to write all these things down. This became the last book in the Bible called the book of Revelation.

Elijah was taken **up** in a fiery chariot to the presence of God!

Jesus descended into hell for three days and three nights as our punishment, but after his resurrection **he ascended upwards** on the Mount of Olive to go be with the father and to sit at the right hand of God.

> "Now that ***he ascended***, what is it but that he also ***descended*** first into the lower parts of the earth?" Ephesians 4:9

In the old testament only select people could come into Gods presence! They had to be **consecrated** or set apart by God such as the **priests**. When God had Moses bring the people into the wilderness to receive the ten commandments at Mount Sinai, **only Moses could come into God's presence. God came down to the mountain top** and **Moses went up to the mountain top:**

> "The LORD ***came down*** on Mount Sinai, to the top of the mountain; and the LORD called Moses to the top of the mountain, and ***Moses went up***. Then the LORD spoke to Moses, 'Go down, warn the people, ***so that they do not break through to the LORD*** to gaze, and many of them ***perish***. 'Also ***let the priests who come near to the LORD consecrate themselves,*** or else the LORD will break out against them. Moses said to the LORD, 'T***he people cannot come up*** to Mount Sinai, for You warned us, saying, 'Set ***bounds*** about the mountain and consecrate it.'" Exodus 19:20-24 (NKJV)

God is Holy and man is corrupt. Man is unable to come into his presence. But the blood sacrifice of Jesus restored man's access to God. God came **down** to earth in bodily form through Jesus and **will bring us up** to God as he brought Moses to the summit of Sinai and showed him his glory and allowed him to enter into his cloud of glory.

When the priests offered animal sacrifices on the altar for the sins of the people, the **smoke always moved upwards**. The symbolism of this upward motion is that our sacrifice comes before God. Jesus rose from the dead and went **upward** to God to present his blood before the mercy seat in heaven.

The Upward Motion of Prayer

Another aspect of the **upward** motion is **prayer**. **It always goes up.** In the holy place was a Golden Altar of Incense that the priest had to keep lit with coals of fire and sweet-smelling incense. They had to make sure the incense was lit before entering through the veil into the Holy of Holies to sprinkle the blood of the yearly sacrifice on the mercy seat of the ark of the covenant. The bible says this altar of Incense represents our prayers.

"Then another angel, who had a golden censer, came and stood at the altar. He was given much ***incense*** to offer, along with the ***prayers of all the saints***, on the golden altar before the throne. And the ***smoke of the incense***, ***together with the prayers of the saints, rose up before*** God from the hand of the angel." Revelation 8:3,4

The smoke of the incense **rising upwards** to God represents our prayers. We need to constantly have the **upward motion of prayer** filling the temple of God in the heavens. As the smoke of the sacrifice rises before God, we see the smoke of incense is like **our prayers and praise going up to him who sits in the highest heights**! David said:

"Let my ***prayer*** be set forth before thee ***as incense***; and the ***lifting up of my hands*** as the evening sacrifice." Psalm 141:2

When Cornelius was approached by an angel and God was about to send Peter to him and his household to hear the gospel, the angel told him:

" ... Thy ***prayers*** and thine alms are ***come up*** for a ***memorial*** before God." Acts 10:4

God looks down at those who pray and listens to the prayers of the righteous!

"For ***the eyes of the Lord*** are on the righteous ***and his ears are attentive to their praye***r, but the face of the Lord is against those who do evil."1 Peter 3:12

The Upward Motion of Praise

Praise is often accompanied with the **lifting up** of holy hands:

"I will therefore that men pray everywhere, ***lifting up holy hands***, without wrath and doubting." 1 Timothy 2:8

"Then Ezra ***blessed*** the LORD the great God. And all the people answered, "Amen, Amen!" while ***lifting up their hands***; then they bowed low and ***worshiped*** the LORD with their faces to the ground." Nehemiah 8:6

"Thus will I bless thee while I live: I will ***lift up my hands*** in thy name." Psalm 63:4

"Let us lift up our heart with our hands unto God in the heavens." Lamentations 3:41

All of us are either going **up or down**. We can't get off the elevator. We have to choose the **binary direction** of not only this life, but the eternal one that lays ahead. Will you choose the wide road on the **left** or the narrow path on the **right**? Will you go **forward** in your walk towards Christ or **backwards**? And will you ultimately arise and go **up** to heaven at his return or will you fall **downward** to await his final judgment? God has made it simple. There are only two choices and **only two directions**! It is up to you which one you decide upon!

Chapter 5 - The Two Consequences - the Binary Code of Blessing and Curses

The Blessings of Obedience

Blessing and Curses are a natural result of obedience or disobedience to God! We will talk about both but first let us look at the blessings of God!

After God gave the Ten Commandments to the nation of Israel, He told them of the **blessings** they would receive if they hearken to His words and kept the statutes of the Law. Nearly every aspect of their lives would be blessed if they listened and obeyed God's word. The condition and the **Blessings** are summarized in *Deuteronomy 28:*

> "And it shall come to pass, ***if*** thou shalt ***hearken*** diligently unto the voice of the Lord thy God, to ***observe*** and to ***do*** all his commandments which I command thee this day, that the Lord thy God will ***set thee on high above all nations of the earth***: And ***all these blessings*** ***shall come on thee, and overtake thee, if thou shalt hearken unto the voice of the Lord thy God.***
>
> Blessed shalt thou be ***in the city***, and blessed shalt thou be ***in the field.***
>
> Blessed shall be ***the fruit of thy body***, and ***the fruit of thy ground***, and the ***fruit of thy cattle***, the increase of thy ***kine***, and the flocks of thy ***sheep***.
>
> Blessed shall be ***thy basket and thy store***.
>
> Blessed shalt thou be ***when thou comest in***, and blessed shalt thou be ***when thou goest out***.
>
> The Lord ***shall cause thine enemies that rise up against thee to be smitten before thy face: they shall come out against thee one way, and flee before thee seven ways***.

> The Lord shall ***command the blessing upon thee in thy storehouses***, and in ***all that thou settest thine hand unto***; and he shall ***bless thee in the land which the Lord thy God giveth thee.***
>
> The Lord shall ***establish thee an holy people unto himself***, as he hath sworn unto thee, if thou shalt keep the commandments of the Lord thy God, and walk in his ways. And ***all people of the earth shall see*** that thou art ***called by the name of the Lord; and they shall be afraid of thee.***
>
> And the Lord shall ***make thee plenteous in goods, in the fruit of thy body, and in the fruit of thy cattle, and in the fruit of thy ground, in the land*** which the Lord sware unto thy fathers to give thee.
>
> The Lord shall ***open unto thee his good treasure, the heaven to give the rain unto thy land in his season, and to bless all the work of thine hand: and thou shalt lend unto many nations, and thou shalt not borrow.***
>
> And the Lord shall ***make thee the head, and not the tail***; and ***thou shalt be above only, and thou shalt not be beneath***; if that thou hearken unto the commandments of the Lord thy God, which I command thee this day, to observe and to do them: And thou shalt not go aside from any of the words which I command thee this day, to the right hand, or to the left, to go after other gods to serve them." Deuteronomy 28:1-14

There are two main Greek words for "**blessing**" in the bible. The first is "***eulogeo***" and it is where we get the word eulogy from. It means *to speak well or praise or acknowledge one's goodness* and can be applied to God or man. It also means *to consecrate or sanctify and to bestow a benefit on someone!*

The second word is "***makarizo***" and means *to prosper, make joyful, happy, full and content*! It has a secondary meaning also which means *to make long, enlarge or increase*. So, the Lords blessings add and bring increase, not decrease!

> "The blessing of the LORD, it maketh rich, and he addeth no sorrow with it." Proverbs 10 22

The Aaronic Blessing!

So essentially blessing means **Holiness** and **Happiness**! When the priesthood was instituted, Moses instructed Aaron and his sons to pronounce blessings over Israel to remind them of these blessings if they were faithful and obedient. This time it was not just about outward blessings on their land and possessions but a more personal blessing upon them with the **protection, favor and presence of God**!

> "Speak to Aaron and his sons, saying, Thus you shall bless the people of Israel: you shall say to them, The Lord ***bless thee***, and ***keep thee***: The Lord ***make his face shine upon thee***, and be ***gracious unto thee***: The Lord ***lift up his countenance upon thee, and give thee peace***!" Numbers 6:23-26 (ESV)

This simple and elegant blessing has been used throughout the centuries long after the sacrifices of the Aaronic priesthood ended. It is still used in Judaism during their services and is also called **the Priestly Blessing**, or Priestly Benediction (*birkat kohanim*), the *Dukhanen*, or the **"raising of the hands**,". The Aaronic Blessing is also used in Catholic, Anglican, and Lutheran liturgy. It is also spoken over the congregation regularly in less liturgical services of many Protestant congregations.

The Beatitude Blessings

Jesus expanded the blessings when he gave the sermon on the mount. This was called the beatitudes. It gets its name from the Latin prefix "**beati**", which translates to be **"happy," "rich," or "blessed**." Now the blessings are not just physical but spiritual and extended to the downcast and **those who suffer**. Here the Greek word for blessed is "makarioi" which means "happy". It may seem strange to declare happiness for suffering situations, but He is showing that God is aware and will bless you despite your situation!

1. "Blessed are ***the poor in spirit,***
   for theirs is the kingdom of heaven.
2. Blessed are ***those who mourn,***
   for they will be comforted.
3. Blessed are ***the meek,***
   for they will inherit the earth.
4. Blessed are ***those who hunger and thirst for righteousness,***
   for they will be filled.
5. Blessed are ***the merciful,***
   for they will be shown mercy.

6. Blessed are ***the pure in heart,***
   for they will see God.

7. Blessed are ***the peacemakers,***
   for they will be called children of God.

8. Blessed are **those who are persecuted** because of righteousness, for theirs is the kingdom of heaven.

9. Blessed are you **when people insult you, persecute you and falsely say all kinds of evil against you** because of me. Rejoice and be glad, because great is your reward in heaven, for in the same way they persecuted the prophets who were before you." Matthew 5:3-12

Jesus is merging the **sufferings** of this life with the **rewards** that follow when we often must endure the hardships of life. The blessing is not in the hardship itself but in the promise of God's recompenses for that suffering. Jesus came into the world knowing that he would greatly suffer at the hands of man and be beaten and scourged and ultimately crucified for no wrongdoing, But Jesus knew **the reward would be your salvation!**

"...who for the *joy* that was set before him ***endured the cross***, despising ***the shame***, and is set down at the right hand of the throne of God." Hebrews 12:2

Jesus set the **joy** of our salvation before him in order to endure the sufferings, the crucifixion and death on the cross. The **reward** of us being redeemed was worth the **suffering**.

The Heavenly Blessings

Paul talks about blessings that are higher than all earthly blessings. There are **Heavenly blessings** or **Spiritual Blessings**!

"***Blessed*** be the God and Father of our Lord Jesus Christ, who ***hath blessed us*** with ***all spiritual blessings in heavenly places in Christ:*** According as he hath ***chosen us*** in him before the foundation of the world, that we should be ***holy and without blame before him*** in love: Having predesignated us unto the ***adoption*** of children by Jesus Christ to himself, according to the good pleasure of his will, To the praise of the glory of his grace, wherein ***he hath made us accepted*** in the beloved. In whom ***we have redemption*** through his blood, ***the forgiveness of sins***, according to the riches of his grace; ... In whom also ***we have obtained an inheritance***, being predestined according to the purpose of him who worketh all things after the counsel of his own will:

That we should be to the praise of his glory, who first trusted in Christ." Ephesians 1:3-12

These spiritual or **heavenly blessings** are **birthright blessings**. They are the blessings of the **inheritance of the children**. In Old testament culture the Jewish children had a birthright blessing. Abraham passed on the birthright to Isaac. Isaac meant to pass on that blessing to Esau his firstborn just before he died but was blind and ended up giving it to Jacob instead.

Jacob had twelve sons and just before he died, he called them together and blessed them and prophesied over their lives and their descendants (Gen. 49)! They received not just a physical inheritance of the land of promise but the blessing or cursing of the father over the children depending on what they did or would do in the future! This is also what Jesus did to the seven churches in Revelations when he pronounces either blessing or curses from heaven upon them depending upon their response to encouragement and correction. He both **praised them for what they were doing right** and **warned them concerning what they were doing wrong.** A father must both encourage his children as well as discipline and correct them!

So, the heavenly blessing is an inheritance blessing because we have been **born again** and **adopted by God as his children.**

"For as many as are led by the Spirit of God, they are the ***sons of God.*** For ye have not received the spirit of bondage again to fear; but ye have received the ***Spirit of adoption***, whereby we cry, ***Abba, Father***. The Spirit itself beareth witness with our spirit, that ***we are the children of God: And if children, then heirs; heirs of God, and joint-heirs with Christ;*** if so be that we ***suffer with him***, that we may be also ***glorified together***." Romans 8:14-17

It is not just blessing on our food and work and possessions, but it is the blessing of being born again and the blessing of our heavenly father to his children. Just as Abraham's blessing gave his children the promise land so we are given a rightful place in heaven and a heavenly abode!

"Let not your heart be troubled: ye believe in God, believe also ***in me. In my Father's house are many mansions***: if it were not so, I would have told you. I go to prepare a place for you. And if ***I go and prepare a place for you***, I will come again, and receive you unto myself; that ***where I am, there ye may be also***." John 14:1-3

The heavenly blessing is the Fathers Blessing and as we are joint heirs with Christ, we have a heavenly home waiting for us along with all the benefits and blessings of heaven! This is a **positional blessing**! It is the blessing of **being adopted and being called the children of God and receiving his heavenly inheritance**.

This is not the earthly blessings of physical **provision, protection and prosperity**. It is the eternal blessings of **salvation, redemption and forgiveness** and the heavenly presence of God! That is the greatest of blessings we could ever have!

The Curses of Disobedience

On the other side of the **binary code** of blessing for obedience is the opposite of blessing! This is **Curses of disobedience**! The **consequence** of right decision, action and obedience lead to blessings but the **consequence** of wrong decision, action and disobedience leads to **curses** upon our life in earth and worse after we die! In the second half of Deuteronomy 28, Moses declares to the people of Israel the **curses** that would come upon them **if they did not obey the laws of God.** This second **binary consequence** of disobedience releases the opposite of blessing:

> "But it shall come to pass, ***if thou wilt not hearken unto the voice of the Lord thy God, to observe to do all his commandments and his statutes*** which I command thee this day; that all these curses shall come upon thee, and overtake thee:
>
> "***Cursed*** shalt thou be in the ***city***, and cursed shalt thou be in the ***field***.
>
> ***Cursed*** shall be ***thy basket and thy store***.
>
> ***Cursed*** shall be ***the fruit of thy body, and the fruit of thy land, the increase of thy kine, and the flocks of thy sheep***.
>
> ***Cursed*** shalt thou be ***when thou comest in***, and cursed shalt thou be ***when thou goest out***.
>
> The Lord shall send upon thee ***cursing, vexation, and rebuke***, in al***l that thou settest thine hand unto for to do, until thou be destroyed, and until thou perish quickly; because of the wickedness of thy doings, whereby thou hast forsaken me.***
>
> The Lord shall make ***the pestilence*** cleave unto thee, until he have consumed thee from off the land, whither thou goest to possess it.
>
> The Lord shall smite thee with a ***consumption***, and with a ***fever***, and with an ***inflammation***, and with an ***extreme burning***, and with the ***sword***, and with ***blasting***, and with ***mildew***; and they shall pursue thee until thou perish.
>
> And ***thy heaven that is over thy head shall be brass***, and the ***earth that is under thee shall be iron.***

> The Lord shall make the ***rain*** of thy land powder and dust: from heaven shall it come down upon thee, until thou be destroyed.
>
> The Lord shall cause thee to be ***smitten before thine enemies:*** thou shalt ***go out one way against them and flee seven ways before them***: and shalt be removed into all the kingdoms of the earth." **Deuteronomy 28:15-25**

The list of curses is far longer than the blessings. It continues to curse the land, the seed, the vineyards, and the trees. It says that your family will be cursed, and you will be taken in war, in sickness, in disease and much more. Is God a mean God for allowing these things to happen to God's people. No! By disobeying God's laws and moving into sin, they now remove themselves from His protection and are allowing Satan and his demons permission to disrupt their lives. **Satan brought the first curse upon himself and his fallen angels** and now he is seeking to "Steal, kill and destroy" those who are no longer under his hedge of protection. *(John 10:10, Job 1:10)*

I encourage you to read the whole chapter of Deuteronomy 28. God gave the nation of Israel the choice of following the Laws of God or disobeying and in so doing it would have brought blessing or curses upon them both individually and as a nation.

The Two Mountains

> "Behold, I set before you this day ***a blessing*** and ***a curse***; ***A blessing, if ye obey*** the commandments of the LORD your God, which I command you this day: And ***a curse, if ye will not obey*** the commandments of the LORD your God, but turn aside out of the way which I command you this day, to go after other gods, which ye have not known. And it shall come to pass, when the LORD thy God hath brought thee in unto the land whither thou goest to possess it, that thou shalt put the ***blessing upon mount Gerizim***, and ***the curse upon mount Ebal***. "Deuteronomy 11:26-29

Moses gave instructions that after the twelve tribes of Israel crossed over the river Jordan and conquered the promise land, they were to go over to two mountains: **Mt. Gerizim** and **Mt. Ebal**. They were to stand atop these adjacent mountains and read aloud the **Blessings** and **Curses** as a reminder of the importance of being obedient to the covenant. After Joshua crossed the Jordan and conquered that part of the land, he took the twelve tribes of Israel and put half of the tribes on Mount Gerizim and half of the twelve tribes on Mount Ebal. (Do you see the principle of binary division?). Between the mountains was the town of Shechem where God first made his covenant with Abraham. Moses put the Levites and the Ark of the covenant between the two mountains (remember the ten commandments were in the ark so the Law was between the blessings and curses!). Joshua and the Levites read the whole Book of the Covenant "with a loud voice" (Deut. 27:14) and **the tribes on Mount Ebal listened to God's curses** for disobedience and **the tribes before Mount Gerizim listened to God's blessings** for obedience. This highly significant prophetic act declares the binary code of obedience to God's word. With the Law in between them they declared the results of obedience or disobedience which would bring forth either blessing or curses. **Mt Gerizim represented the blessings** and **Mt Ebal represented the curses.** (Interestingly Israel would later be divided into the northern tribe of Israel and southern Tribe of Judah under Kings Jeroboam and Rehoboam. More on this later!)

We are either blessed for adhering to God's word or cursed for rejecting it. Our country has been extremely blessed because the puritans and first Europeans came over for religious freedom and to seek a Christian homeland. The first laws of this country were the ***Mayflower Compact*** a strong Christian covenant with God! Even our constitution was based upon the scriptures and God's law. We have been blessed like no other nation because of it, but in recent times we have not only embraced atheistic and evolutionary thoughts that deny our Creator but have rejected his laws. Adultery is commonplace. **Murder** is accepted now through abortion and Euthanasia and now is being pushed more and more! Politicians **lie** and **steal** from the people and we applaud gay rights and transgenderism. We have turned the blessing into a curse. Can we expect no less a punishment than Israel did when she forgot her God?

> "The Lord will send on you ***curses***, confusion, and frustration in all that you undertake to do, until you are destroyed and perish quickly on account of the evil of your deeds, because you have forsaken me" (Deuteronomy 28:20). (ESV)

Israel would later turn from God, follow the world around them by embracing false Gods, and embracing sin. Thus, God allowed the curses to come upon them including the promise of the curse of being taken into captivity by their enemies. This is precisely what happened when Babylon took them captive and destroyed the temple. Even after they repented and were brought back to the land, they later rejected Christ and as he prophesied, the temple, the city and the nation were destroyed within one generation by the Romans. God was not being cruel to Israel. He was simply removing his blessings and hedge of protection and the enemy came in. When we disobey God, we remove His blessing and give Satan permission to bring upon the curse, which is a result of sin.

Mountain of Slavery or Mountain of Freedom

The six tribes on **Mount Ebal, the mount of cursing**, included **Gad** and **Asher**, Jacob's children by **Zilpah the slave** and the tribes of **Dan**, and **Naphtali**, sons of **Bilhah the slave**. So, these were the children of Jacob's concubines (Leah and Rachel's handmaids and servants). They were on the mountain of curses because they represented servitude! **Reuben**, though he was one of Leah's legitimate sons, was **cursed** because he had sexual relations with Bilhah, his father's concubine. (Also, Zebulun, may have been on the cursed mountain for failing to drive out the Canaanites living in Kitron and Nahalol).

Those on **Mount Gerizim, the mount of blessing,** are **Simeon**, **Levi**, **Judah**, **Issachar**, and **Joseph**. These are the **natural children of Jacob's lawful wives, Leah and Rachel** (Gen. 35:23-26). Here we see the symbolism of the division of **the free from the slave**. Obedience sets us free (John 8:32) but disobedience enslaves us.

Paul touches on this as he declares that we are either children of God through obedience to Him, or we are slaves to sin!

> "Because you are his sons, God sent the Spirit of his Son into our hearts, the Spirit who calls out, "Abba, Father." So, ***you are no longer a slave***, but ***God's child***; and since you are his child, God has made you also ***an heir***. Formerly, when you did not know God, you were ***slaves*** to those who by nature are not gods. But now that you know God—or rather are known by God—how is it that you are turning back to those weak and miserable forces? ***Do you wish to be enslaved by them all over again?***" Galatians 4:6-9 (NIV)

> "Do you not know that if you present yourselves to anyone as ***obedient slaves, you are slaves of the one whom you obey***, either of sin, which leads to death, or of obedience, which leads to righteousness?" Romans 6:16 (ESV)

The Curse of the Law

The bible talks about the **curse of the law** because the ten commandments tell us what is right and what is wrong but does not give us the ability to do what is right and avoid what is wrong.

> "For as many as are of the works of the **law** are under the **curse**: for it is written, Cursed is every one that continueth not in all things which are written in the book of the law to do them." Galatians 3:10

There is a curse in the Law because it condemns us when we have not the ability to obey it by nature. Our flesh and our sin nature gravitate to disobedience and therefore to sin and thus places a curse upon our lives. The answer is **a new nature.** When we are born again by the Spirit of God, we can walk not according to the flesh but according to the spirit and keep the law.

"But if ye be led of the Spirit, ye are not under the law." Galatians 5:18

This is because God is love and the love of God is shed abroad in our hearts by the Holy spirit and **love helps us keep the law.**

"Let no debt remain outstanding, except the continuing debt to love one another, for ***whoever loves others has fulfilled the law.*** The commandments, "You shall not commit adultery," "You shall not murder," "You shall not steal," "You shall not covet," and whatever other command there may be, are summed up in this one command: "Love your neighbor as yourself." Love does no harm to a neighbor." Romans 13:8-10 (NIV)

With love, the curse is broken, and the blessing of grace is that we have been given God's love in measure within our hearts and if we yield to that love we will automatically fulfill the law and break the curse! **The sin nature** has been replaced with **God's nature**. Yes, we still must deal with the flesh, the world, and the Devil, but keeping the law comes by obedience to our spirit, not our flesh, and to the Holy Spirit, not our old nature!

"There is therefore now ***no condemnation*** to them which are in Christ Jesus, who ***walk not after the flesh***, but ***after the Spirit***."
Romans 8:1-39

The Blessing and Curses of the Tongue!

One other aspect of the binary principle of **blessing and cursing** has to do with our **tongues,** or rather our speech! The bible says that the tongue has the power of **life** and **death**!

"***Death and life are in the power of the tongue:*** and they that love it shall eat the fruit thereof." Proverbs 18:21

Our words have power! They can hurt someone or bless someone. They can lift someone up or they can tear someone down. Our words can affect people and they can affect ourselves. They can defile people and they can defile ourselves. Our words are powerful containers that can edify and build up those around us or they can destroy them.

The power of the press is a great example. Certain tabloids have ruined the careers of many by exposing the truth to someone's hurt. They have often done the same to others by falsify and lying about someone. Many have committed suicide because of bullies or verbal abuse. Others could never recover from fake news and false accusations.

Part of the curse of the tongue is the ability of people to **lie**. We live in a society where fake news is a large part of the mainstream media and the social network. One of the Ten Commandments says **"Thou shalt not bear false witness."** Yet because of the wickedness of men's hearts and because men are prone to lie, God later stipulated that if someone is accused of something, **two or more witnesses** must come forth to collaborate the truth! *(Deuteronomy 19:15, Matthew 18:15-20)*

The Pharisees could not find fault with Jesus, so the bible says that they tried to hire people to give false testimony and lie about him, but the false witnesses could not get their stories straight!

> "And the chief priests and all the council sought for ***witness*** against Jesus to put him to death; and found none. For ***many bare false witness against him***, but their ***witness agreed not together***. And there arose certain, and ***bare false witness against him***, saying, We heard him say, I will destroy this temple that is made with hands, and within three days I will build another made without hands. Bu***t neither so did their witness agree together***."
> Mark 14:55-59

Can you imagine standing before God on judgment day after falsely accusing Jesus for money in order to crucify Jesus. They were no better than Judas and will receive a similar judgment!

The Curse of Profanity

Isn't it interesting that profanity is also called cursing or cussing? The word cussing is just a variant of the word cursing. When you cuss you curse.

The word profanity comes from the Latin word "profanare" which simply means to desecrate or make what is holy, unholy. The word originally had to do with the Commandment against profaning the name of the Lord or "taking his name in vain". One dictionary says that ***"Profanity is language irreverent toward God or holy things, covering especially all oaths that, literally interpreted, treat lightly the attributes or acts of God."*** Later it was used as it is now to describe any language that was crude, coarse, lewd, vulgar, and blasphemous.

James talks much about the power of the tongue as being a small thing with great power to steer and direct one's life!

> "We all stumble in many ways. Anyone who is never at fault in ***what they say*** is perfect, able to keep their whole body in check. When we put bits into the mouths of horses to make them obey us, we can turn the whole animal. Or take ships as an example. Although they are so large and are driven by strong winds, they are steered by a very small rudder wherever the pilot wants to go." James 3:2-4 (NIV)

Here we see that if we control the tongue, we can control the whole body as a horse's bit can direct the whole body of a horse and direct it where you want it to go. The other analogy is the rudder or steering wheel (helm), that is able to steer a giant ship though it is but a small part. It goes on to say:

> "Even so the tongue is ***a little membe***r, and boasteth great things." Behold, how great a matter ***a little fire*** kindleth! And ***the tongue is a fire, a world of iniquity:*** so is the tongue among our members, that it defileth the whole body, and setteth on fire the course of nature; and it is set on fire of hell." James 3:5-6

James compares the tongue as a small fire that can quickly grow and consume much. Just a few words can burn others and set our course to hell. The tongue is untamable and utterly defilable to us and others. It can be poison to the hearers.

> "But the tongue can no man tame; it is an unruly evil, full of deadly poison." James 3:8

We have the awesome ability to bless or curse with our speech, yet too many mix the two:

> "Therewith ***bless we God,*** even the Father; and therewith ***curse we men,*** which are made after the similitude of God. Out of the same mouth proceedeth ***blessing and cursing.*** My brethren, these things ought not so to be. Doth a fountain send forth at the same place ***sweet water*** and ***bitter***? Can the fig tree, my brethren, bear olive berries? either a vine, figs? so can no fountain both yield ***salt water*** and ***fresh***." James 3:9-12

I have seen and find it so sad when so-called Christians praise God on Sunday and then curse and talk dirty at work on Monday!

The Curse of Balaam Turned Blessing

There was a man in the old testament that was hired by a king to bring a curse upon the nation of Israel. His name was Balaam and the King of

Moab whose name was Balak brought Balaam to a high mountain where the Israelites were camped in the valley. Balaam raised his hands to curse the nation, but God would not let him and instead he blesses Israel. King Balak takes him to another mountain and Balaam tried again but again God would not let him curse his people and instead blesses him. This naturally infuriated Balak. So, he took him to a third mountain, but when Balaam stood on it the spirit of God came on him and blessed Israel for the third time. King Balak said:

> "I summoned you to ***curse*** my enemies, but instead you have ***blessed*** them these three times." Numbers 24:10 (NIV)

You cannot curse whom God blesses. God said he will bless those who bless Israel and curse those who curse Israel!

> "I will ***bless those who bless you***, And I ***will curse him who curses you***!" Genesis 12:3 (NKJV)

Though Balaam could not directly curse Israel he showed Israel how to curse themselves by disobeying God. But more on that later!

Generational Curses

There are some indications in the scriptures that there are some curses that are inherited. These are called generational curses.

> "The LORD is longsuffering, and of great mercy, forgiving iniquity and transgression, and by no means clearing the guilty, ***visiting the iniquity of the fathers upon the children unto the third and fourth generation.***" Numbers 14:18

> "Keeping mercy for thousands, forgiving iniquity and transgression and sin, and that ***will by no means clear the guilty; visiting the iniquity of the fathers upon the children, and upon the children's children, unto the third and to the fourth generation***." Exodus 34:7

Perhaps this is not an actual indictment upon the children for sins of the fathers or grandfathers but a natural result of the influence of wickedness upon the seed of man. Regardless anyone can be free from the generation curse when they turn wholly to the Lord and then the blessing will overshadow the curses! We must all actually be held responsible for our **own** sins!

> "The soul that sinneth, it shall die. The son shall not bear the iniquity of the father, neither shall the father bear the iniquity of the son: the righteousness of

the righteous shall be upon him, and the wickedness of the wicked shall be upon him." Ezekiel 18:20

Nor are we to hold one man accountable for anther's actions. God warned Israel that no one should be put to death for another generation's sin!

"The fathers shall not be put to death for the children, neither shall the children be put to death for the fathers: ***every man shall be put to death for his own sin.*** " Deuteronomy 24:16

The effects of our conduct and speech leads to either blessing or curses upon ourselves. This **Binary system of Curses and Blessings** again shows the **division of right and wrong** along with its consequences. Ultimately, we bring a curse upon our life when we depart from the Lord and look to serve the flesh or the ways of man!

"Thus saith the LORD; **Cursed** [be] the man that trusteth in man, and maketh flesh his arm, and whose heart departeth from the LORD." Jeremiah 17:5

Chapter 6 - The Two Covenants - the Binary Code of God's Law & Grace

The Two Testaments

The Bible is divided into **two binary sections**, the **Old testament** and the **New Testament**. The word testament means **Covenant.** God has made **two main covenants** with man. First, In the Old testament after the flood, man fell into idolatry, worshiping a myriad of false Gods and forgot their real Creator. The world's nations moved into polytheism so God decided he would establish one nation to be a witness to all the others that there was only one God! He established monotheism through the nation of Israel. He would separate Abraham from his relatives, move him to another country which he would give him and promised that out of his loins would come a nation that would be as numeric as the stars and the sands of the sea! **This covenant was between Abraham and his seed** as long as they kept it.

> "No longer will you be called Abram; your name will be Abraham, for I have made you a father of many nations. I will make you very fruitful; I will make nations of you, and kings will come from you. ***I will establish my covenant as an everlasting covenant between me and you and your descendants after you*** for the generations to come, to be your God and the God of your descendants after you. The whole land of Canaan, where you now reside as a foreigner, I will give as an everlasting possession to you and your descendants after you; and I will be their God." Then God said to Abraham, "As for you, you must keep my covenant, you and your descendants after you for the generations to come." Genesis 17:5-9 (NIV)

A covenant requires more than a promise. It also requires a **sign** or a **supernatural miracle** confirming that it is of God. The miracle was that Abraham was a hundred years old when he had Isaac. Abraham's wife, Sarah was ninety.

> "When ***Abram*** was ***ninety-nine years*** old, the LORD appeared to him and said, "I am God Almighty; walk before me faithfully and be blameless. Then I

> will make my ***covenant*** between me and you and will greatly increase your numbers." Abram fell face down, and God said to him, "As for me, this is ***my covenant with you***: You will be the ***father of many nations***." Genesis 17:1-4 (NIV)

They initially **both** scoffed at the idea and laughed at its impossibility!

> "Abraham fell face down; he ***laughed*** and said to himself, "Will a son be born to a man a hundred years old? Will Sarah bear a child at the age of ninety?" Genesis 17:17 (NIV)

> "Now Abraham and Sarah were old and well stricken in age; and it ceased to be with Sarah after the manner of women. Therefore ***Sarah laughed within herself,*** saying, After I am waxed old shall I have pleasure, my lord being old also? And the LORD said unto Abraham, ***Wherefore did Sarah laugh,*** saying, Shall I of a surety bear a child, which am old? ..." Genesis 18:11-13

When God speaks, it is no laughing matter, but as impossible as it seems all things are possible with God. Though Abraham initially laughed, he latter believed God and it was reckoned to him as righteousness (*Rom. 4*). Though the old covenant with Abraham was made through faith the continued covenant with his people was made through Moses when God gave them the Ten Commandments. This was called the Law. More on that later!

As the covenant with Abraham was established through a miraculous birth in old age through the birth of Isaac so would the **New Testament** be established through a miraculous birth! In **the New Covenan**t God would also establish it with a miraculous birth which he prophesied in Isaiah:

> "Therefore, the LORD himself will give you a sign: ***The virgin will conceive and give birth to a son*** and will call him Emmanuel." Isaiah 7:14 (NIV)

This was fulfilled with Mary and the virgin birth of Jesus Christ.

> "She will give birth to a son, and you are to give him the name Jesus, because he will save his people from their sins." All this took place ***to fulfill what the LORD had said through the prophet:*** "The ***virgin*** will conceive and give birth to a son, and they will call him Emmanuel" (which means "God with us")." Matthew 1:21-23 (NIV)

The Old Covenant was also established with the physical sign of circumcision. Circumcision was a sign in the flesh of Abraham's seed showing that they were under the covenant that God made with Abraham! Every male child in Israel would undergo this cutting of the flesh to mark their separation and consecration to God!

"This is my ***covenant*** with you and your descendants after you, the covenant you are to keep: ***Every male among you shall be circumcised***. You are to undergo circumcision, and it will be the ***sign of the covenant between me and you***. For the generations to come every male among you who is eight days old must be circumcised, including those born in your household or bought with money from a foreigner—those who are not your offspring. Whether born in your household or bought with your money, they must be circumcised. ***My covenant in your flesh*** is to be an everlasting covenant." Genesis 17:10-13 (NIV)

The **sign** however in the new covenant is **a new heart.** When a person believes in Jesus Christ and is born again the bible says he is a New creation and old things are passed away. He has not just been forgiven but has been given **a new nature!**

"For circumcision is indeed profitable if you keep the law; but if you are a breaker of the law, your circumcision has become uncircumcision. Therefore, if an uncircumcised man keeps the righteous requirements of the law, will not his uncircumcision be counted as circumcision? And will not the physically uncircumcised, if he fulfills the law, judge you who, even with your written code and circumcision, are a transgressor of the law? For ***he is not a Jew who is one outwardly, nor is circumcision that which is outward in the flesh; but he is a Jew who is one inwardly; and circumcision is that of the heart, in the Spirit, not in the letter***; whose praise is not from men but from God.." Romans2:25-29 (NKJV)

The Prophet Ezekiel predicted the day when God would change the heart of man under the new covenant!

"I will give you a new heart and put a new spirit within you; I will take the ***heart of stone*** out of your flesh and give you a ***heart of flesh***." Ezekiel 36:26

Again, we see the binary pattern of two hearts. One of **stone** and one of **flesh**. This is not merely the replacing of the hardened heart, but it is a contrast of stone and flesh. The Law or Ten Commandments were written on stone. It was a riged law that simply pointed to sin whereas the heart of flesh is a heart where the law of God is written in your heart by God not just on stone tablets! The law and circumcision were given to the Jews, but the new nature is given to all who believe:

"Indeed, when ***Gentiles***, who do not have the law, do by nature what the law requires, they are a law to themselves, even though they do not have the law, since they show that ***the work of the law is written on their hearts***, their ***consciences*** also bearing witness, and their thoughts either accusing or defending them." Romans 2:14-15

Jesus simplified the Law by explaining that the Ten Commandments can be broken down into its binary form from ten to **two commandments** which have to do with the heart not just outward obedience.

"And, behold, a certain lawyer stood up, and tempted him, saying, Master, what shall I do to inherit eternal life? He said unto him, What is written in the law? how readest thou? And he answering said, Thou shalt ***love the Lord thy God with all thy heart***, and with all thy soul, and with all thy strength, and with all thy mind; ***and thy neighbour as thyself***. And he said unto him, ***Thou hast answered right: this do, and thou shalt live.*** " Luke 10:25-28

Paul understood the **two covenants** were **the Law and Love**. By walking in God's love, you will automatically keep the law by nature of its virtue:

"The commandments, "You shall not commit adultery," "You shall not murder," "You shall not steal," "You shall not covet,"and whatever other command there may be, are summed up in this one command: "***Love*** your neighbor as yourself. "Love does no harm to a neighbor. Therefore, ***love is the fulfillment of the law.*** " Romans 13:8-10 (NIV)

Isaac and Ismael- Types of the Two Covenants!

The Apostle Paul in the book of Galatians shows the that the old Testament Law is binding and enslaves you to its riged system whereas the law of Love sets us free. Here he shows the contrast of the **two** under the symbolism **of the two children** of Abraham. One was born from a **slave or servant to Sarah** and the other was **naturally born to Sarah**. The first was a **human effort** to fulfill the promise of God and the other was **God's fulfillment** of his promise to Abraham!

"Tell me, you who want to be under the law, are you not aware of what the law says For it is written that Abraham had ***two sons*** (***Isaac and Ismael***), ***one by the slave woman*** and ***the other by the free woman***. His son by the slave woman was born according to the ***flesh***, but his son by the free woman was born as the result of a divine ***promise***. These things are being taken figuratively (symbolically): The women represent ***two covenants.*** One covenant is from ***Mount Sinai*** (where the law was given) and bears children who are to be slaves: This is Hagar. Now Hagar stands for Mount Sinai in Arabia and corresponds to the present ***city of Jerusalem***, because she is in slavery with her children. But the ***Jerusalem that is above*** is free, and she is our mother. For it is written: "Be glad, barren woman, you who never bore a child; shout for joy and cry aloud, you who were never in labor; because more are the children of the desolate woman than of her who has a husband. Now you, brothers and sisters, like Isaac, are children of promise. At that time the son born according to the flesh persecuted the son born by the power of the Spirit. It is the same now. But what does Scripture say? ***"Get rid of the slave woman and her son, for the slave woman's son will never share in the inheritance with the free woman's son."*** (Words of Sarah to Abraham – Genesis 21:10) Therefore, brothers and sisters, we are not children of the ***slave woman***, but of the ***free woman***." Galatians 4:21-31 (NIV)

Here we see **the binary code of freedom and slavery**. He speaks of the **natural Jerusalem** where men are **slaves to sin** and this world and of the **New Jerusalem** where **all men are free**! Sarah's Servant was given to Abraham to try to bring forth the promise. **Ismael** was born of the slave and Abraham wanted to leave his inheritance to him, but God told him no. He said a natural son would come, the child of the covenant, the child of promise. **Isaac** finally was born and fulfilled the promise of God in his covenant to Abraham. Out of Abraham Isaac and Jacob the nation of Israel would arise to give witness and testimony to the true and Living God. Paul said these two sons represent **the two covenants. The old and the new; the law and the spirit.** One was slavery and one was freedom. Abraham was instructed to cast out the child of the slave so that the true son could receive the inheritance of God's promise.

The bible calls these two covenants "**the Law of the spirit of Life** and the **Law of Sin and death.**

"For ***the law of the Spirit of life*** in Christ Jesus hath made me free from ***the law of sin and death.***" Romans 8:2

The law of Life is stronger than the law of Sin and Death. It sets one free. It is a **higher covenant. A greater covenant.** The covenant God made with Abraham was temporary and fixed to his seed. But the new covenant in Christ is eternal and for all mankind!

"But in fact the ministry Jesus has received is as ***superior*** to theirs as ***the covenant of which he is mediator*** is ***superior*** to the old one, since ***the new covenant*** is established on ***better promises***. For if there had been nothing wrong with that first covenant, no place would have been sought for another.... 13 By calling this covenant "***new***," he has made ***the first one obsolete***; and what is obsolete and outdated will soon disappear." Hebrews 8:6,7,13 (NIV)

"By so much was Jesus made a surety of a ***better*** testament." Hebrews 7:22

The Covenant of the Law and the Covenant of Grace.

"For sin shall not have dominion over you: for ye are not under the ***law***, but under ***grace***." Romans 6:14

The old testament and the new testament are covenants, or binding pledges between **two** parties. The first came by Moses as a covenant between God and Israel and was sealed by the giving of the Law or ten commandments. The Law however, simply pointed out right from wrong to bring us back to the knowledge of good and evil. It did not remove sin but simply pointed out to man that we were under sin.

"Knowing that a man is ***not justified by the works of the law***, but by the ***faith of Jesus Christ***, even we have believed in Jesus Christ, that we might be justified by the faith of Christ, and not by the works of the law: for by the works of the law shall no flesh be justified." Galatians 2:16

The second covenant came through Jesus and is between God and all of mankind but binding only to those who have obtained salvation through faith in Christ. Though we did not merit it Jesus obtained salvation for us and now justification does not come through keeping the Law but by faith in Jesus Christ. This is called grace! The binary system is the contrast of **works** and **grace**, human effort and divine intervention!

"For by ***grace*** are ye saved through faith; and that ***not of yourselves:*** it is the gift of God: Not of works, lest any man should boast." Ephesians 2:8,9

Chapter 7 - The Two Positions - the Binary Code of Truth and Error

The Long War against Truth

The dichotomy of Truth is that it is unalterable yet can be manipulated. It is incorruptible yet people can change it, it is pure, yet it can be diluted, and it is absolute yet can be deniable!

The disastrous event of the war in heaven was a war between the **truth and a lie**. God only knows truth and Jesus said that he was the "Way, the **Truth** and Life!" (John 14:6). Satan introduced lies by deceiving the angels and later by lying to Adam and Eve in the garden! Jesus called Satan a liar and the Father of lies!

> "You belong to your father, the ***devil***, and you want to carry out your father's desires. He was a murderer from the beginning, ***not holding to the truth***, for ***there is no truth in him***. When he ***lies***, he speaks ***his native language***, for ***he is a liar*** and the ***father of lies***." John 8:44 (NIV)

I like how the NIV puts it that lying is his native language! Satan is a liar and is at war with the truth. A lie questions the truth! It distorts the truth. It waters the truth down and even blinds men to the truth.

One thing my mom told me as a kid and always stuck with me was: "I ***would rather know the truth no matter how bad, than a lie know matter how good***!" It kept me honest!

Paul said however, that in the end time this lying will be the work of the Antichrist. He will lie and deceive and sadly **people would rather believe a lie than know the truth.**

> "...Even him, whose coming is after the working of ***Satan*** with all power and signs and ***lying wonders***, And with all ***deceivableness*** of unrighteousness in them that perish; because ***they received not the love of the truth***, that they might be saved. And for this cause God shall send them ***strong delusion***, that ***they should believe a lie:*** That they all might be ***damned*** who ***believed not the truth***, but had pleasure in unrighteousness." 2 Thessalonians 2:8-12

The ultimate end results of lies are not just deception, but destruction. The binary war is a war not of just good vs evil but truth vs error! Those who do not hold to the truth and perpetuate falsehood are in danger of the wrath of God.

> The ***wrath of God*** is being revealed from heaven against all the godlessness and wickedness of people, ***who suppress the truth*** by their wickedness, Romans 1:18 (NIV)

One of the clearest signs of men preferring a lie to the truth is the increase of the acceptance of the LGBTQ movement. Same sex marriage is now legal, and the gay lifestyle is not only acceptable, but many churches employ gay ministers even though the bible clearly states God's position on the matter:

> "For this cause God gave them up unto ***vile affections***: for even their ***women did change the natural use into that which is against nature:*** And likewise also the ***men, leaving the natural use of the woman, burned in their lust one toward another; men with men working that which is unseemly,*** and receiving in themselves that recompense of their error which was meet. And even as they did not like to retain God in their knowledge, God gave them over to ***a reprobate mind***, to do those things which are not convenient; Being filled with all unrighteousness, fornication, wickedness, covetousness, maliciousness; full of envy, murder, debate, deceit, malignity; whisperers, Backbiters, haters of God, despiteful, proud, boasters, inventors of evil things, disobedient to parents, Without understanding, covenant breakers, ***without natural affection***, implacable, unmerciful: ***Who knowing the judgment of God***, that they which commit such things are ***worthy of death***, not only do the same, but ***have pleasure in them that do them***." Romans 1:26-32

The willful war against the truth of God's word has come to its fruition with deceptions such as evolution, abortion, transgender, homosexuality, and other lies. An atheistic and Antichrist generation questions the validity of God's word. It started with Satan saying "Hath God said?" and now men would rather believe a lie than the truth because truth convicts of sin! Truth uncovers and reveals. Truth settles the matter. Truth wins the argument but only if truth is accepted and believed!

Turning to the truth has far more benefits if people will embrace it. Only the truth sets you free from lies and deception.

> "And ye shall know the ***truth***, and ***the truth shall make you free***." John 8:32

God only sees truth and He sees beyond our lies. God has never lied to man and thus his word is the ultimate truth! Truth separates you from the false and insincere. There is a holiness to the truth! Truth sanctifies and consecrates your life to God

"*Sanctify* them through ***thy truth***: thy ***word is truth***." John 17:17

Satan has deceived men through **two great lies**. He has convinced man that either there is **no God** or that there are **many ways to God**. Atheism has taken root in our colleges and robbed the Christian upbringing of many. Most scientist deny the bible and do not believe in God! Scientists are supposed the be the most learned and smartest people but Paul says"

"Professing themselves to be wise, they became ***fools***!" Romans 1:22

Atheists and evolutionists try to utilize reason to rationally do away with God and dispel the need for a Creator, but God says of their so-called intellect that they are simply fools:

"The ***fool*** hath said in his heart, there is no God." Psalm 53:1

It is simply foolish to challenge the truth and believe a lie. The bible says that God's word is truth. To impose **man's opinions over God's declarations** is the ultimate foolery. And as it has been said "A fool has been fooled."

The binary principle of Truth vs. Lies is called a **spirit** in the Bible. They are opposing forces of God's Spirit or Demonic spirits called t**he Spirit of Truth** and the **Spirit of Error!**

"We are of God: he that ***knoweth*** God ***heareth*** us; he that is not of God heareth not us. Hereby know we ***the spirit of truth***, and the ***spirit of error***." 1 John 4:6

The ability to discern Truth from Error requires two things **Knowing** and **Hearing**. You must **know** God by being born again and receiving Jesus as your sin sacrifice. Once you know God you can begin to **hear** God and then the **truth** is revealed by his Spirit.

Jesus told the disciples after being with them for three and a half years that he was going to leave them and go back to the Father. He had taught them truth but now that he was leaving them, he promised someone would come to continue leading them in the truth!

"However, when he, ***the Spirit of truth***, is come, he will ***guide you into all truth***: for he shall not speak of himself; but whatever he shall hear, that shall he speak: and he will show you things to come." John 16:13

Truth comes not from **reasoning** but from **revelation**. It is **supernaturally revealed by the Holy Spirit.** The Holy Spirit is now our teacher and tutor and guides us through revelation into **"all" truth.** What a precious gift, to be given the unction of the Holy Spirit to be our teacher and tutor and to unveil God's truths to us!

Spiritual Blindness and Spiritual Insight!

Have you ever known someone who was blind? I have a cousin who was born blind. Imagine the difficulty comprehending the world around you. Their world is a world of darkness, a world without color and a world limited and hard to understand. This is how the spiritual world is to all men who are living in sin. Salvation opens our eyes and enables us to comprehend God and his invisible kingdom. The bible says:

> "But if our gospel be ***hid***, it is hid to them that are lost: In whom the ***god of this world*** hath ***blinded the minds of them which believe not,*** lest the ***light*** of the glorious gospel of Christ, who is the image of God, ***should shine unto them***. For we preach not ourselves, but Christ Jesus the Lord; and ourselves your servants for Jesus' sake. For ***God, who commanded the light to shine out of darkness,*** hath shined in our hearts, to give ***the light of the knowledge of the glory of God in the face of Jesus Christ.*** 2 Corinthians 4:3-4

Remember in the beginning God did not create darkness he simply created light to shine out of the darkness. This is illumination and symbolic of the revelation God gives to open our eyes after **Satan has blinded our understanding of truth.**

Paul before his conversion, was called Saul and he was going around arresting and condemning Christians until one day God appeared to him as a bright light. This **blinded** Paul as a symbol of his **spiritual blindness**. He had to be led around by the hand. God sent a man named Ananias to pray for him and the Bible says **scales fell off his eyes and God restored his eyesight**. What a wonderful example of what God does for us spiritually when we become born again!

Israel could not comprehend Jesus as the Messiah because they were expecting a warrior king to deliver them from the Romans, not suffer on a cross and die for mankind. Paul said

> "For I would not, brethren, that ye should be ignorant of this mystery, lest ye should be wise in your own conceits; that ***blindness*** in part is happened to Israel, until the fullness of the Gentiles be come in. "Romans. 11:25

This was not a physical blindness but a spiritual one. Jesus said:

> "For judgment I came into this world, so ***that those who do not see may see, and that those who see may become blind***." John 9:39 (NAS)

Faith opens up spiritual sight and doubt makes us blind to the truth! More on that later.

Parallels of the Miracles of Jesus

Now is probably a good time to talk about the spiritual parallels to the physical miracles of Jesus.

> "God anointed Jesus of Nazareth with the ***Holy Spirit and power***, and how he went around ***doing good*** and ***healing*** all who were under the ***power of the devil***, because God was with him." Acts 10:38 (NIV)

A couple of observations here. Jesus was a healer. Often **His healings in the Physical realm also were a type of Jesus healing in the Spiritual Realm**. We know that Jesus healed many **blind people.** In one case he spit on the ground and made mud and told the man that was born blind to wash his eyes in the Pool of Salome and he was instantly healed. Perhaps in this case Jesus was doing a creative miracle and had to actually create new eyes for the man born blind; after all he is the Creator and made all things (Col.1:16) and if God made Adam out of the dust of the ground Jesus could take dust from the ground and add water and make new eyes.

The point here is that just as Jesus healed physical eyes he heals and opens spiritual eyes. As he healed people who were physically paralyzes and heals those who are spiritually paralyzed. He healed the deaf and they could hear, and he enables us to hear the voice of God. He took away leprosy and removed the blight of sin from our souls. The parallel is compelling.

The other point is we see the word "***power***" used twice in this sentence. God anointed Jesus with the **power by the Holy Spirit** to heal and then it says he healed all those under **the power of the Devil**. The Power of God is the Greek word "***Dunimus***" meaning: "*force, miraculous ability or might.*' It implies supernatural strength or might. The other word Power is the Greek word "***katadunasteuw***" meaning "*Ones dominion or oppression*". The King James translates it all "*who were oppressed by the devil.*"

So, Jesus who healed and cast out devils with Gods power was delivering people from the power of Satan's dominion and oppression. Again, the binary principle of two **forces: one binds and oppresses, and one delivers. One imprisons and one sets free**. So, the outward healings and deliverances of Jesus also represent his power over all the power of the enemy physically and spiritually. (Luke 10:19)

Worshiping in Truth or Error

Remember when we talked about the two mountains and the curses and Blessings on Mount Ebal and Mount Gerizim? Next to these two mountains was the town of Samaria. The Jews hated the Samaritans because they were a mixed race of Jews and Gentiles! Normally all travelers avoided this area and went way out of their way to go around it! That is why the disciples where surprised when Jesus decided to go through Samaria. The disciples went to get food and Jesus encountered the "Woman from Samaria."

Let's backtrack a bit. After King Solomon died the nation of Israel was **divided** into **two** kingdoms. The **northern part was called Israel** and was ruled by a wicked man named Jeroboam and the **southern part was called Judah** was ruled by someone not much better, King Rehoboam.

Just as the divisions on the two mountains predicted, the tribes of Israel would be **divided,** and some would fall under the curse of disobedience. The northern tribes departed from Yahweh and fell into idolatry.

The southern kingdom had Jerusalem and the Temple. Jeroboam the king of the northern tribes set up his own capital in the city of Shechem. Remember Shechem was the town between Mount Ebal and Mount Gerizim the place between the curses and blessings. Jeroboam cursed the people because he went beyond the sin of the Golden Calf that Aaron made in the wilderness, for he set up ***two*** golden calves to be worshiped. He put one in Bethel, and one in the city of Dan, and forbade the people to go up yearly to Jerusalem, as they were instructed to do by God during the feasts! He also made idolatrous shrines in the high places and set up a false priesthood that did not include Levites, which defied God's command. He had the people offer sacrifices on his own altars and on his own made up feast days! In other words, he created a counterfeit religion and defiantly did exactly what the curses warned him not to do.

God sent a prophet to warn him that a descendant of David of the house of Judah named Josiah would destroy his altar. However, rather than being convicted, Jeroboam stretched out his hand trying to arrest the prophet and his hand withered right before him. Jeroboam asked the prophet to restore his hand and the prophet did and left, but Jeroboam still refused to repent.

So, what does this all have to do with the woman at the well in Samaria? Well Samaria became the second capital of the Northern kingdom. At one point the whole northern tribe was called Samaria.

This is why the Jews in Jerusalem and other parts hated the Samaritans. They represented the rebellious and idolatrous people who even at Jesus day were still **falsely** worshiping God on Mt Gerizim. This is why the woman at the well said the following.

> "Sir, I see that you are a prophet. Our ancestors ***worshiped*** on this ***mountain***, but you say that the place where people must worship is in ***Jerusalem***." Jesus said to her, "Woman, believe me, the hour is coming when you will ***worship the Father neither on this mountain nor in Jerusalem. You worship what you do not know***; ***we worship what we know***, for salvation is from the Jews. But the hour is coming, and is now here, when the ***true worshipers will worship the Father in spirit and truth, for the Father seeks such as these to worship him. God is spirit, and those who worship him must worship in spirit and truth.*** " The woman said to him, "I know that Messiah is coming" (who is called Christ). "When he comes, he will proclaim all things to us." Jesus said to her, "***I am he***, the one who is speaking to you." John 4:19-26 (NIV)

Here we see Jesus makes a distinction between **true worship** and **false worship**. The woman was referring to the false idol worship on the mountain which Jesus said, was why they worshiped a God they do not know. In Jerusalem there was at least an outward worship of the true God, but Jesus was prophesying of a time when after His resurrection men would be filled with the Spirit of God and could worship in Spirit and truth. Only by knowing God personally through Jesus Christ could we really appreciate and worship him as our Creator and Redeemer.

> "We are of God: he that ***knoweth*** God ...Hereby know we ***the spirit of truth***, and the ***spirit of error***." 1 John 4:6

False worship is worshiping a God "you do not know"; that is without intimate relationship. This is **religious and outward** where true worship is **inward in the heart** and in Truth! **False worship** can pertain to church services and gatherings without personally knowing God and his salvation. That is why we have so many **false religions and cults.** But we who **know** the Lord personally through Jesus Christ can truly worship him by the Spirit and in truth!

Knowledge vs. Ignorance

The binary code of **knowledge and ignorance** started in the garden. The first couple **knew God** but were ignorant of good and evil. They were living an **innocent** but happy life communing with God daily. A child initially does not know or understand the difference between good and evil and parents do all they can to shelter the children from the evils of the world. But ultimately, they will grow up to see the evils of the world and lose that innocence! God kept **the knowledge of evil** from them yet knew that his righteous nature had to allow them the choice to understand what was hidden or to continue in happy ignorance. So, he placed the **tree of the knowledge of Good and Evil** in their midst and gave them the choice to be happy through ignorance or unhappy by knowing the realities of sin and evil!

But now, it's ironic that Satan wants to **hide** the truth of God's existence and love from mankind. Jesus came to unveil the truth to us, but Satan has blinded those who desire not the truth. Ignorance is blinding. It affects the mind (understanding) and the heart (belief.)

"Having the ***understanding darkened***, being alienated from the life of God through the ***ignorance*** that is in them, because of the ***blindness of their heart***." Ephesians 4:18

Ignorance of truth is destructive. Satan comes to kill, steal, and destroy so he tries to keep Gods truth from each generation.

"My people are ***destroyed*** for ***lack of knowledge***: because t***hou hast rejected knowledge,*** I will also reject thee, that thou shalt be no priest to me: seeing thou ***hast forgotten*** the law of thy God, I will also forget thy children." Hosea 4:6

As a child is somewhat accountable until he comes of age, so God at one time overlooked our ignorance. But now if we know we are sinners and that Christ has died for our sins, he will hold us accountable!

"And the ***times of this ignorance*** *God winked at; but now commandeth all men everywhere to repent." Acts 17:30*

Chapter 8 - Accuse or Excuse - the Binary Code of our Conscience

Knowing Right from Wrong!

When Adam and Eve ate the forbidden fruit, it opened their eyes. They developed a conscience and knew right from wrong. This is why they hid from God. They knew that they disobeyed God! Conscience is the ability to feel guilt when one does wrong. That does not remove guilt, it hopefully leads to repentance. Conscience is explained in the new testament:

> "They show that the work of the law is written on their ***hearts***, while their ***conscience*** also ***bears witness***, and their conflicting ***thoughts accuse*** or even ***excuse*** them!" Romans 2:15 (ESV)

A person's conscience is their **inner spirit bearing witness** to the **law of right and wrong** that has been **written on our hearts**. Then our thoughts will either **accuse us** (telling us that we are guilty) or **excuse us** (saying we are not guilty).

> "The spirit of man is the lamp of the Lord, ***searching*** all his innermost parts." Proverbs 20:27 (ESV)

A Defiled and Seared Conscience

As Christians, we are to walk in the spirit and follow our conscience. The bible says that if we listen to our heart and obey it, we have a "good conscience". On the other hand, rejecting the voice of one's conscience will destroy your faith.

"The aim of our charge is ***love that issues from a pure heart*** and a good conscience and a sincere faith... holding faith and a good ***conscience***. By ***rejecting*** this, some have made ***shipwreck of their faith***."1 Timothy 1:19 (ESV)

We have the choice to listen to our conscience or not. We can either be sensitive to that inner voice within us or we can choose to ignore it! If we continue to refuse to listen to our conscience the bible says our conscience will become defiled!

"To the pure, all things are pure, but to the defiled and unbelieving, nothing is pure; but ***both their minds and their consciences are defiled***." Titus 1:15 (ESV)

One can come to a point where they quit listening to their conscience and harden their heart to the conviction of their spirit. The bible refers to this as having your heart seared or cauterized.

"Now the Spirit speaketh expressly, that in the latter times some shall ***depart from the faith***, giving heed to seducing spirits, and doctrines of devils; Speaking lies in hypocrisy; ***having their conscience seared with a hot iron***."
1 Timothy 4:1-2

Remember when we talked earlier about a **heart of flesh** and a **heart of stone?** A stony heart is one who no longer has a conscience! Pharaoh hardened his heart before God and refused to let the Israelites go until he had no choice and even after letting them go, he changed his mind and pursued then into the desert until he lost his army in the Red Sea!

The nation of Israel had collectively **hardened their heart** towards God and backslid as a nation. Paul said of them:

"The Holy Spirit spoke the truth to your ancestors when he said through Isaiah the prophet: 'Go to this people and say, "You will be ever hearing but never understanding; you will be ever seeing but never perceiving." For this people's ***heart has become calloused;*** they ***hardly hear with their ears***, and they have ***closed their eyes.*** Otherwise they might see with their eyes, hear with their ears, understand with their hearts and turn, and I would heal them." Acts 28:27 (NIV)

Other versions describe the calloused heart as "hardened", waxed Gross", "become stubborn" and "become dull"

Notice how the hardened heart affects the **seeing and hearing**? God is not talking about the physical binary ears or eyes but the spiritual perception and understanding. They have closed their **eyes** to the truth and can no longer **hear** the voice of conscience that speaks!

From Guilt to Salvation

Pain is a necessary function of the human body. The nervous system connects to the brain and uses a process called nociception. A pain receptor called a nociceptor responds to damaging or potentially damaging stimuli by sending "possible threat" signals to the spinal cord and the brain. If the brain perceives the threat as credible, it creates the sensation of pain to direct attention to the body part, so the threat can hopefully be alleviated.

Guilt is not pleasant, but necessary to show us what is right or wrong, sometimes even before we act on something. Burning yourself on a stove will hopefully prevent you from doing it again. **Doing something wrong and feeling guilty will hopefully keep you from doing it again.** This is conscience! In another chapter we will talk about remembering and forgetting and much of this will be made clearer! **Guilt's** purpose is to lead to **conviction** which in turn should lead us to **repentance** and **forgiveness** end then a **clear conscience!**

> "Now I rejoice, not because you were grieved, but because your ***grief led to repentance.*** For you were grieved as God willed, so that you didn't experience any loss from us. For godly grief produces a repentance not to be regretted and ***leading to salvation***, but worldly grief produces death." 2 Corinthians 7:9-10 (HCSB)

Guilty Conscience vs Clear Conscience!

Conscience is binary in the sense that we can either have a **clear** conscience or a **guilty** one! Having guilt and not releasing that guilt is often called having a "guilty conscience"! The purpose is to bring us to repentance!

If, however we are free from guilt it is said that we have a "Clear conscience (Heb. 13:18, 1 Tim. 3:9 ESV)

We are to strive to continually have a good conscience towards both God and man.

"So I always take pains to have a ***clear conscience*** toward both God and man." Acts 24:16 (ESV)

Under the old testament the people of Israel would offer the blood sacrifices of animals as a covering for their sins. This would give them a clear conscience **for a year** before God!

In the new covenant of Christ, it is the shedding of His blood that grants forgiveness of sins an gives a clean conscience **forever** before God!

"How much more will the ***blood of Christ***, who through the eternal Spirit offered himself without blemish to God, ***purify our conscience*** from dead works to serve the living God." Hebrews 9:14 (ESV)

Baptism a Sign of a Good Conscience Before God

Sometimes we need an **outward expression** of an **inner work** to confirm the heart of man. Baptism does not save but it can outwardly express our inner relationship with Christ and our redemption. Thus, being plunged into water and rising out of it symbolizes the grave, and by it, identifies with the death, burial, and resurrection of Christ. There is a mystery attached to this work that somehow adds to a clear conscience with God. Perhaps it's the reality of the death of the old man and its sinful nature and the rising into a resurrected life free from guilt. This is why Peter said:

"There is also an anti-type which now saves us—***baptism*** (not the removal of the filth of the flesh, but the answer of ***a good conscience*** toward God), through the resurrection of Jesus Christ." 1 Peter 3:21 (NKJV)

Conscience is the effect of guilt on us. I used to tease people and say ***if you feel guilty than you probably are***. Guilt can often be put on us by men, but ultimate real guilt is based on if our heart condemns us or not, Gods power of forgiveness is greater than our own self guilt:

"Little children, let us not love in word or talk but indeed and in truth. By this we shall know that we are of the truth and reassure our heart before him; for ***whenever our heart condemns us***, God is greater than our heart, and he knows everything. Beloved, if our ***heart does not condemn us***, we have confidence before God." 1 John 3:18-21 (ESV)

Confession of sin and repentance of heart lead to forgiveness and thus cleanses us from guilt!

> "If we confess our sins, he is faithful and just to ***forgive*** us [our] sins, and to ***cleanse*** us from all unrighteousness." 1 John 1:9

Since guilt is personal condemnation, only the power of God's personal forgiveness can remove that condemnation.

> "There is therefore now ***no condemnation*** to them which are in Christ Jesus, who walk not after the flesh, but after the Spirit." Romans 8:1

Guilt from Accusation

Satan is called the **accuser of the brethren**. He seeks to constantly remind you of your sins to make you feel guilty. But you have to remember SATAN IS NOT YOUR CONSCIENCE! He has no right over you as a Christian. The one who rebelled against God and is eternally damned and condemned by God certainly has no right to condemn **you**. It is said that when Satan reminds you of your past you just remind him of his future!

Also, men often try to impose guilt and condemnation on other people! Remember the woman caught in adultery that the religious Scribes and Pharisees brought to Jesus to test him. According to the law she was to be stoned. They asked Jesus what his answer was, hoping to trap him, but Jesus knelt down and started writing in the sand. He probably was writing a list of his accusers' sins in front of them:

> "So when they continued asking him, he lifted up himself, and said unto them, ***He that is without*** sin among you, ***let him first cast a stone at her***. And again he stooped down, and wrote on the ground. And they which heard it, ***being convicted by their own conscience***, went out one by one, ***beginning at the eldest, even unto the last***: and Jesus was left alone, and the woman standing in the midst. When Jesus had lifted up himself, and saw none but the woman, he said unto her, Woman, where are those thine accusers? hath no man ***condemned*** thee? She said, No man, Lord. And Jesus said unto her, ***Neither do I condemn thee***: ***go, and sin no more***." John 8:7-11

It is interesting that as Jesus wrote in the sand, the eldest left first, then the youngest. The older you get the more you are aware of what you have done wrong in your life. Often the youth have a weaker sense of guilt until time allows it to accumulate in the heart.

It does not matter what men think of your sins. They have their own to worry about! It is only before God that you must stand, and it is only what He thinks that matters. Jesus dispelled the human accusers and brought the matter before her and God. He chose to forgive her and instructed her to sin no more. One of my favorite scriptures is:

> "What shall we then say to these things? If ***God*** be ***for us***, ***who*** can be ***against us***?" Romans 8:31

WHO means nothing! **GOD** means everything! Who will always be against us, but God will always be for us!

Chapter 9 - The Two Realms – the Binary Code of the Spirit and Matter

The Twofold Nature of Man!

"That which is born of the flesh is ***flesh***, and that which is born of the Spirit is ***spirit***." John 3:6 (ESV)

Adam was a twofold binary being. He was flesh and spirit! First, he had a body made from the dust of the earth. In other words, God used matter and the physical elements of the ground to create the outer shell of man. But then God breathed into him and he became a living soul! He was not alive until the breath of God entered him and now the inner soul was created! He was now Flesh and Spirit. The flesh was cursed after the fall and this dual nature along with the curse upon the flesh passed on to Adam's children and their descendants!

"Wherefore, as by ***one man sin*** entered into the world, and death by sin; and so ***death passed upon all men***, for that all have sinned." Romans 5:12-13 (KJV)

When Adam sinned, the ground was **cursed**. So, **matter and the physical world** became subject to **death and decay**. Since Adams body was made from the ground, his **body was also cursed**. Just as God told him that the day, he ate of the forbidden fruit he would be subject to death. The **spirit of man is eternal** because it is the breath of God, but **the body will die** because it is made from the earth and now the law of entropy will take over the body. The law of entropy works in all matter. Contrary to evolution over time things fall apart and get worse, not better.

But the body is simply our outer shell. That outer shell is often referred to in the bible as **a tent** because we are not our bodies; we **dwell** in a body.

"For we know that if the ***tent*** that is our ***earthly home is destroyed,*** we have a building from God, a house not made with hands, ***eternal*** in the heavens. For in this tent ***we groan, longing to put on our heavenly dwelling***, if indeed by putting it on we may not be found naked. For while we are still in this tent, we ***groan***, being burdened—not that we would be unclothed, but that we would be further clothed, so that what is ***mortal*** may be swallowed up by life. He who has prepared us for this very thing is God, who has given us the ***Spirit*** as a guarantee. So we are always of good courage. We know that ***while we are at home in the body we are away from the Lord,*** for we walk by faith, not by sight. Yes, we are of good courage, and we would ***rather be away from the body and at home with the Lord.*** So, ***whether we are at home or away, we make it our aim to please him***. For we must all appear before the judgment seat of Christ, so that ***each one may receive what is due for what he has done in the body, whether good or evi***l."2 Corinthians 1:10

While we are in the **body** we are **away from the Lord**! Because of our **sinful flesh we cannot enter heaven**. But the time will come when we die if we are redeemed, we will be with him but away from our bodies. Paul said.:

"We are confident, I say, and willing rather to be ***absent from the body,*** and to be ***present with the Lord***." 2 Corinthians 5:8

Because of the sin nature, there is a **war** going on between the flesh and the spirit. The spirit seeks to follow one's conscience and do what is right, but the flesh because of the curse, seeks its own desire and **wars** against the soul:

"Beloved, I urge you as sojourners and exiles to abstain from the passions of the ***flesh***, which ***wage war against your soul."*** 1 Peter 2:11 (ESV)

"But I see in my members another law ***waging war*** against the law of my mind and making me captive to the law of sin that dwells in my members." Romans 7:23 (ESV)

Their natures oppose each other because the spirit of man has a moral code written within it, but the flesh seeks its own ways.

"The human ***spirit*** is the lamp of the LORD that ***sheds light*** on one's ***inmost being***." Proverbs 20:27 (NIV)

The law is written on our hearts, but the flesh seeks not to follow it. Thus, they are contrary to each other and conflict with each other.

"For the ***flesh desires*** what is ***contrary*** to the ***Spirit***, and the ***Spirit what is contrary to the flesh***. They are in ***conflict*** with each other, so that you are not to do whatever you want. " Gal.5:17 (NIV)

Here we clearly see the evidence of eating from the Tree of the knowledge of **good and evil**. The **flesh** now cannot follow Gods laws so is inherently **evil,** but the **Spirit** seeks to do **good**! This is why Paul said there is no good in his flesh but only evil due to sin:

> "For I know that ***nothing good dwells in me, that is, in my flesh***. For I have ***the desire to do what is right, but not the ability to carry it out.*** For I do not do the ***good*** I want, but the ***evil*** I do not want is what I keep on doing. Now if I do what I do not want, it is no longer I who do it, but ***sin that dwells within me***." Romans 7:18-20

The dictates of the flesh are self-centered. It seeks its own desires and gratification. There is **no motivation of love in the flesh.** The spirit or soul of man is different. Because God is love and our spirits are the essence of the breath of God, it has the capacity to love. This is the contrary and opposing nature of the binary man. We must learn to be governed by our higher nature and not the flesh. We have a body, but it must be under subjection to the Spirit.

> "But I say, ***walk by the Spirit,*** and you will not gratify the desires of the flesh." Galatians 5:16 (ESV)

> "For if you live according to the flesh you will die, but ***if by the Spirit you put to death the deeds of the body, you will live***." Romans 8:13 (ESV)

The Works of the Flesh

> "Now the works of the flesh are evident: ***sexual immorality, impurity, sensuality, idolatry, sorcery, enmity, strife, jealousy, fits of anger, rivalries, dissensions, divisions, envy, drunkenness, orgies, and things like these***. I warn you, as I warned you before, that those who do such things will not inherit the kingdom of God." Galatians 5:19-21:

The **binary nature** of **flesh** and **spirit** conduct itself differently from each other. Sowing to the flesh reaps works of unrighteousness but sowing to the spirit produces the very nature of God. Again, we see the garden tree with its dual nature has taken root in the heart of man producing opposing results.

God clearly shows us in the scripture above **that the dictates of the flesh** transfer to **three governing realms of man:**

1.<u>**Physical Realm**</u>: This includes ***drunkenness (and physical addictions such as drug addiction), sexual immorality, impurity, sensuality, and orgies (sex with multiple partners). This also includes Adultery, fornication, homosexuality, and bestiality!***

The consequences to physical sin can affect the physical body! **Sowing to the flesh will cause one to reap from the flesh**. This could include diseases, miscarriage, sickness, cancer, and even physical death:

> "Be not deceived; God is not mocked: for whatsoever a man ***soweth***, that shall he also ***reap***. For ***he that soweth to his flesh*** shall ***of the flesh reap corruption***; but he that ***soweth to the Spirit*** shall of the Spirit reap life everlasting." Galatians 6:7-8

2.<u>**Emotional Realm**</u>**:** ***strife, jealousy, anger, envy, divisiveness, and contention!***

Surprisingly, these are considered the works of the Flesh though they are seated in our thought realm and emotions. That is because they are triggered by the selfish nature of the flesh.

> "For where you have ***envy*** and ***selfish ambition***, there you find ***disorder*** and ***every evil practice***." James 3:16

3.<u>**Demonic Realm**</u>: such as ***sorcery, witchcraft, and idolatry.***

These are obviously anti-God and satanic in nature. Worshiping Satan or any other false God is a work of the sin nature which opens one up to the demonic realm and will lead to eternal consequences. God's Wrath will ultimately come upon those who have turned from their Creator to worship another!

> "Therefore, ***put to death*** your members which are on the earth: ***fornication, uncleanness, passion, evil desire, and covetousness, which is idolatry***. Because of these things the <u>***wrath of God***</u> is coming upon the sons of disobedience, in which you yourselves once walked when you lived in them. But now you yourselves are to ***put off*** all these: ***anger, wrath, malice, blasphemy, filthy language out of your mouth.***" Colossians 3:5-8 (NKJV)

The works of the flesh is the outward expressions and actions of a cursed body and must be brought under subjection to the Spirit of man and God!

The Fruit of the Spirit

The spirit produces not just good works put the very nature of God. Again, the scriptures tie this back to the Edenic Tree symbolism of fruit produced by a tree!

> "But the ***fruit*** of the Spirit is ***love, joy, peace, patience, kindness, goodness, faithfulness, gentleness, self-control***; against such things there is no law. And those who belong to Christ Jesus have crucified the flesh with its passions and desires. If we live by the Spirit, let us also keep in step with the Spirit." Galatians 5:22-25

The flesh produces the curse of matter, but the Spirit releases the blessings of God and gives us a new nature with our inner man now being governed by the Holy Spirit. The fruit of God's nature comes by abiding in his Son and allowing him to produce the fruits of righteousness in your life.

> "I am the vine, you are the branches; he who ***abides in Me*** and I in him, he ***bears much fruit,*** for apart from Me you can do nothing." John 15:5

The Carnal Man and Spiritual Man

Not only does mankind have a dual or binary nature, (natural man who is unsaved and Spiritual man who is born again), but Christians can unfortunately also be binary in nature. The Bible talks about the **Carnal Christian**, who is saved but backslidden or still led by the flesh, (thus immature or undeveloped spiritually) and the **Spiritual Christian** who is governed by the spirit and is mature in their faith and growth! The Apostle Paul said:

> "And I, brethren, could not speak unto you as unto ***spiritual***, but as unto ***carnal***, even as unto ***babes in Christ***. I have fed you with ***milk***, and not with ***meat***: for hitherto ye were not able to bear it, neither yet now are ye able. For ye are yet ***carnal***: for whereas there is among you ***envying, and strife, and divisions,*** are ye not ***carnal***, and walk as men? For while one saith, I am of Paul; and another, I am of Apollos; ***are ye not carnal***? Who then is Paul, and who is Apollos, but ministers by whom ye believed, even as the Lord gave to ev-

ery man? I have planted, Apollos watered; but God gave the increase." 1 Corinthians 3:1-6

Immaturity along with envy, strife and division were signs of a carnal Christian being led by the flesh rather than the Spirit. God wants the believer to grow up by feeding on the word of God.

"Like newborn babies, long for the ***pure milk of the word***, so that ***by it you may grow*** in respect to salvation."1 Peter 2:2

A natural man who is not born again has difficulty discerning spiritual things.

"But the ***natural man*** does not receive the things of the Spirit of God, for they are foolishness to him; nor can he know them, because they are spiritually discerned." 1 Corinthians 2:14 (NKJV)

Jesus requires us to walk in the Spirit and not in the flesh. This means we are to be led by our inner man and the Holy Spirit and not the outer man. We also must "put our mind on" the things of the spirit and not on the flesh. Thus, we must listen to our inner voice and be governed by our conscience.

"For God has done what the law, weakened by the ***flesh***, could not do. By sending his own Son in ***the likeness of sinful flesh*** and for sin, he ***condemned sin in the flesh***, in order that the righteous requirement of the law might be fulfilled in us, ***who walk not according to the flesh but according to the Spirit.*** For ***those who live according to the flesh set their minds on the things of the flesh***, but ***those who live according to the Spirit set their minds on the things of the Spirit***. For ***to set the mind on the flesh is death,*** but ***to set the mind on the Spirit is life and peace***. For ***the mind that is set on the flesh is hostile to God***, for it ***does not submit to God's law***; indeed, it cannot. ***Those who are in the flesh cannot please God***. You, however, are not in the flesh but in the ***Spirit***, if in fact the Spirit of God dwells in you." Romans 8:3-9

Overcoming the flesh requires us to live by the spirit! We must reckon the old man dead, (that is the old life), and walk in newness of life!

"And those who belong to Christ Jesus have ***crucified the flesh with its passions and desires***." Galatians 5:24 (ESV)

"Therefore, we are ***buried with him by baptism into death***: that like as Christ was raised up from the dead by the glory of the Father, even so we also should ***walk in newness of life***." Romans 6:4

Walking in the flesh and allowing the body to rule over the spirit is just what the devil seeks man to do, but this will never please God!

> "Those who are in the flesh cannot please God." Romans 8:8 (ESV)

> "Let not ***sin*** therefore reign in your ***mortal body***, to make you obey its passions. Do not present your members to sin as instruments for unrighteousness but present yourselves to God as those who have been brought from death to life, and your members to God as instruments for righteousness." Romans 6:12-13 (ESV)

The Old man and the New Man

> "That ye ***put off*** concerning the former conversation ***the old man,*** which is corrupt according to the deceitful lusts; And be renewed in the spirit of your mind; And that ye ***put on the new man***, which after God is created in righteousness and true holiness." Ephesians 4:22-24. (ESV)

> "***Do not lie to*** one another, since you have ***put off the old man*** with his deeds, and have ***put on the new man*** who is renewed in knowledge according to the image of Him who created him," Colossians 3:9,10 (NKJV)

Here we see the two binary natures: the **old man** and t**he new man**! The old man is the old sinful self, alienated from God and doomed to destruction. But after trusting in God and being born again we have become a new man redeemed in the nature of Christ and able to be led by the Spirit rather than the flesh. Just as we chose our wardrobe, we can choose to take off the deeds of our old nature and put on the deeds of the new man, made righteous in Christ! The distinction between the old and the new is unfathomable. What we were and what we now have become are light years apart in comparison. We are not just a **restoration** but a **recreation.** We are not like a patched up and newly restored antique car but rather we are completely remade in God's image and supernaturally recreated in our spiritual man! Old things have become new!

> "Therefore, if any man be in Christ, he is a ***new creature***: ***old*** things are passed away; behold, all things are become ***new***." 2 Corinthians 5:17

We know what we were, and we know what we have become but it does not yet appear what we shall be. For if the new creation is glorious how much more glorious shall the final transformation be when we will receive glorified bodies in preparation for heaven!

Corruptible vs. Incorruptible.

God has also promised us **a new glorified body** that will equally encompass both the spiritual and physical realm. The Bible says while we Christians dwell in this physical body, we long for our spiritual body.

> "And not only the creation, but we ourselves, who have the first-fruits of the Spirit, ***groan inwardly*** as we wait eagerly for adoption as sons, ***the redemption of our bodies***." Romans 8:23 (ESV)

The new bodies we will receive will be totally free of the curse. They will not be subject to death but will be eternal as they are changed from corruptible to incorruptibly!

> "Behold, I shew you a mystery; We shall not all sleep, but we shall all be ***changed***, In a moment, in the twinkling of an eye, at the last trump: for the trumpet shall sound, and the dead shall be raised incorruptible, and we shall be ***changed***. For this ***corruptible must put on incorruption***, and this mortal must put on immortality. 54So when this corruptible shall have put on incorruption, and this mortal shall have put on immortality, then shall be brought to pass the saying that is written, Death is swallowed up in victory." 1 Corinthians 15:51-54

The binary code of the spirit and matter pits the outer man against the inner man; the flesh against the spirit, the desire to seek good or selfishness and the curse of disobedience against the blessing of following God. Ultimately with Gods help of His word and the Holy Spirit we can overcome the dictates of the flesh and follow the higher power of the spirit.

Chapter 10 - The Two Orders - the Binary Code of God's Priesthood

The Order of Aaron and Melchizedek

When we think of Priests, we often conjure up pictures of men with long robes and long beards or perhaps men with backward collars standing in a pulpit giving long sermons or benedictions. But God initiated a priesthood in behalf of man to stand as an **intercessor between man and God**. Because God is Holy, and man is sinful it was necessary initially to create a body of consecrated men to be intercessors to God in behalf of man.

There are **two orders** of priesthood in the Bible. **The Aaronic Priesthood** and t**he Melchizedek Priesthood.** The first pertains to the earthly priesthood of man and the other the heavenly priesthood of Christ!

The Aaronic Priesthood

Aaron, the brother of Moses was the first high priest over Israel. His role as a spokesman before Pharaoh in Egypt was even a preparation and type of his priesthood that would come in the wilderness as well as a prophetic type of intercessor priest for the people! If you remember Aaron accompanied Moses to Egypt and became his spokesman before Pharaoh because Moses was reluctant to do the speaking.

> "And Moses said unto the LORD, O my Lord, I ***am not eloquent,*** neither heretofore, nor since thou hast spoken unto thy servant: but ***I am slow of speech, and of a slow tongue.***" Exodus. 4:10

The Greek word for ***slow*** is "**kabed**" and means "hesitant, hard or difficult" so it is very possible that Moses stammered or had a speech impediment. Regardless, Moses tried to get out of the job, so God told him to take Aaron with him.

> "And the anger of the LORD was kindled against Moses, and he said, Is not Aaron the Levite thy brother? I know that ***he can speak well***. And also, behold, he cometh forth to meet thee: and when he seeth thee, he will be glad in his heart. And thou shalt speak unto him and put words in his mouth: and ***I will be with thy mouth, and with his mouth,*** and will teach you what ye shall do. And ***he shall be thy spokesman unto the people***: and he shall be, even he shall be to thee instead of a mouth, and thou shalt be to him instead of God." Exodus 4:14-16

Here we see a prophetic word from God that Aaron would be a spokesman to the people. Part of the work of a priest is to speak in behalf of God to the people.

He not only spoke before Pharaoh, but in the wilderness, he often spoke in behalf of God to the children of Israel. Later when God instructed them to build the tabernacle, He set up **Aaron and his two sons to be priests** who would offer up the sacrifices for the people. The Hebrew word for Priests is "Kohan" and they were always descendants of Aaron and his sons, Eleazar, Ithamar, Nadab and Abihu. The two eldest sons, **Nadab and Abihu** were killed by God when they offered up *"strange fire"* (ex. 30:9) upon the Altar of Incense and were thus consumed by fire! We do not know what they did but they were required to take the Censer (a gold container on chains) and fill it with coals from the Altar of Burnt offering (containing the blood of the sacrifice) and then mix it with a specifically made Incense and then place it on the altar in the Holy Place to bring fragrance before God. Perhaps they did not use the coals from the altar or used their own homemade incense. Regardless, they did not follow God's laws and the promise was that those who offered up strange fire would be cut off (killed).

Nadab and Abihu were both childless so the priesthood or "Kohanim" would now be the descendants of Aaron's younger sons, **Eleazar and Ithamar**. Interestingly we see here that the first priesthood was divided in two by two sets of brothers. **Two were disobedien**t in ministry and the other **two faithful.** Two were cursed and lost their inheritance of a lineage of priests and the other two would have their descendants move into the priesthood for generations. Later we see another **binary system of the Priesthood** when God sets of the ministry of the Levites.

The Levites

When God set up the Tabernacle, he called **the rest of Aaron's tribe, the Levites to also be priests** and serve as part of the religious work in the Tabernacle. After the sins of the Golden calf, Moses asked who was for the Lord and the tribe of Levi stood with Moses (Exodus 32:26–29). God rewarded them for their faithfulness by having them assist Aaron and his sons, the priests. However, while Aaron and his sons ministered in the spiritual realm of the tabernacle, the Levites ministered in the physical things.

When the tabernacle (or Tent of Meeting) was moved during those decades in the wilderness it was the Levites who broke town the Tents and walls and carried them from place to place. They also set it back up and dealt with all the physical aspects of the ministry. They would attend to the holy vessels and furnishings of the tabernacle and later in the temple (Both Solomon's and Herod's!) All priests were to be Levites, according to the Law, but not all Levites were priests.

During Jesus day the priesthood of the temple was again divided into **two binary groups**: the **Pharisees** and **Sadducees** (There was a third group called the Essenes which were a monastic group but broke away from the temple service.) The two divisions of the priesthood had major doctrinal differences but served together to represent the Jewish faith. Today we have basically **two** groups that have major doctrinal differences in Christianity: **Catholics** and **Protestants**. It's amazing how the binary pattern continues to emerge.

Interestingly in the New testament we see only **two offices** mentioned in the church, **The Elder (or bishop)** and **the Deacon.** The elders' function as priests and deal with the spiritual aspects of the church but the Deacons like the Levites take care of the physical aspects of the church. The word **elder** means "**overseer, controller, guardian or ruler.**" But the word **deacon** mean "**servant**" This is not a demeaning title, but simply a functional one.

The office of **Deacons** was established in the early church due to **physical needs** not being met in the church! It also was one of the first contentions between the **Jewish Christians** and the **Gentile Christians.**

> "And in those days, when the number of the disciples was multiplied, there arose a murmuring of the Grecians against the Hebrews, because their widows

were neglected in the daily ministration. Then the twelve called the multitude of the disciples unto them, and said, It is not reason that we should leave the word of God, and serve tables. Wherefore, brethren, look ye out among you seven men of honest report, full of the Holy Ghost and wisdom, whom we may appoint over this business. But we will give ourselves continually to prayer, and to the ministry of the word." Acts. 6:1-4

The distinction is clear. Though this has changed much in many churches today, originally the deacons would "***serve tables***" or minister about the physical aspects of ministry while those who were set in as leaders and elders of the church would devote themselves to: "***the Word of God and Prayer***"! Thus, the ministry of the old testament priesthood would foreshadow the ministry of the Church.

Let me at this point clarify the Jewish distinction between the Priests and the Levites. At times, the Levites are certainly called priests but initially the priesthood was Aaron and his sons who were from the tribe of Levi. Later all the descendants of Aaron would be considered priests, After the golden calf incident. God separated the whole tribe of Levi to be sanctified as a priest of a lower order. The Levites aided the priests (sons and descendants of Aaron) and were caretakers of the tabernacle. The tribe of Levi was unique in that they were separated as the firstborn before God (Num. 3:41) and thus sanctified and set apart for the work of God! They did not receive land in Canaan but were provided for by the tithe of the other tribes. Though the Levites were indeed called priests in title they **functioned** differently than the Aaronic priests! The priests were made holy, the Levites were made clean; the priests were anointed and washed, the Levites were sprinkled; the priests were given new garments, the Levites washed theirs; blood was applied to the priests, but was waved over the Levites. Like the priests they could approach the Tent of Meeting whereas the rest of the twelve tribes could not.

However, it was the Aaronic priests who would offer up sacrifices and enter the holy place as well as enter the Holy of Holies once a year on the Day of Atonement. Even the New testament makes the distinction between the Priests and the Levites. The priesthood had become corrupted because at one-point priests were no longer always descendants of Aaron because during the captivity many were simply appointed to that position. The Levites however were always from the tribe of Levi!

It says concerning the parents of John the Baptist that both his Parents were descendants of Aaron and his father was a high priest who went into the Holy of Holies and was greeted by an angel (Luke 1). But when John the Baptist was baptizing in the wilderness it says:

"And this is the record of John, when the Jews sent ***priests*** and ***Levites*** from Jerusalem to ask him, Who art thou?"

Several times in the New Testament we see the **Levites** are distinguished from the **priests**. Even Jesus made this distinction.

In the parable of the good Samaritan it was a **priest** and a **Levite** that passed by the wounded Samaritan and refused to help (Luke 10 25-37)

The High Priest

The Aaronic priesthood also had a **second division** that functioned in both the tabernacle and the Temple. There was the regular **priest** but there were also **the High Priest!** While his sons were priests, **Aaron** himself **functioned as a high priest.** Later on after Aaron died a priest was appointed to be the high priest! Though there was an outer court in both the Tabernacle and the Temple, the Sanctuary was divided into two areas, the Holy Place, and the Holy of Holies. The priests could go into the Holy Place but only the **High priest was allowed into the Holy of Holies.** The role of the High Priest was to **once a year** offer a sacrifice to atone for all the sins of the entire Israelite community (Lev. 16:34). This was called Yom Kippur or the Day of Atonement. He would enter the Holy of Holies and sprinkle the blood of the animal sacrifice on to the mercy seat of the ark of the Covenant!

"But only ***the high priest*** entered the inner room, and then only once a year, and never without blood, which he offered for himself and for the sins the people had committed in ignorance." Hebrews 9:7 (NIV)

This **High Priest** was also a type of Christ who went into heaven and presented his blood as a sacrifice for our sins!

"Neither by the blood of goats and calves, but ***by his own blood*** he ***entered in once into the holy place***, having obtained ***eternal redemption*** for us. For if the blood of bulls and of goats, and the ashes of an heifer sprinkling the unclean, sanctifieth to the purifying of the flesh: How much more shall ***the blood of Christ***, who through the eternal Spirit offered himself without spot to God, purge your conscience from dead works to serve the living God?" Hebrews 9:12-14

"After the same manner also he took the cup, when he had supped, saying, this cup is ***the new testament in my blood:*** this do ye, as oft as ye drink it, in remembrance of me." 1 Corinthians 11:25

Again, we see the twofold binary symbol of forgiveness. Under the **Old Covenant** the Blood of Animals **covered** sin. But under the **New Covenant** Christs blood **cleanses** sins.

"But if we walk in the light, as he is in the light, we have fellowship one with another, and ***the blood of Jesus Christ his Son cleanseth us from all sin.*** " 1 John 1:7

The early church also had a **Presiding elder** that oversaw the church. Today we call this function **Pastors or Shepherds**. The first church in Jerusalem had many elders and the twelve Apostles but we see clearly that **James** was the **presiding elder** who had been appointed by Jesus and led the early church there. This is why James gave the final decision at the First Council at Jerusalem concerning the gentiles converts (Acts 15:13-20) and why Paul went down after he got saved to meet "James and the elders" (Acts 21:18) In a sense **James represented the high priest** as the presiding elder.

The Melchizedek Priesthood.

After the **Aaronic Priesthood** we have the **Melchizedek Priesthood. The Melchizedek Priesthood** is an office that applies only to **Christ the Jewish Messiah!** Melchizedek is a mysterious character that Abraham met after he rescued his nephew Lot from being captured from Sodom after five kings fought four others in the area. He is only mentioned twice in the old Testament. Melchizedek came out to greet Abraham after Abraham defeated the four invading kings and rescued Lot:

"And ***Melchizedek king of Salem*** brought forth ***bread and wine***: and he was the ***priest of the most high God.*** And he blessed him, and said, Blessed be Abram of the most high God, possessor of heaven and earth: And blessed be the most high God, which hath delivered thine enemies into thy hand. And ***he gave him tithes of all.*** " Genesis 14"18-20

Abraham did not care about the spoils. He just wanted his nephew back, but it is interesting that Abraham gave a tithe of the spoils to Melchizedek. **Tithing goes to God**! This passage is also the **first** use of the word **priest** in the bible, so **the Melchizedek order actually came before**

the Aaronic priesthood. This is because the heavenly priesthood existed long before the earthly priesthood!

It is also interesting that Melchizedek offered **bread and wine** to Abraham which Jesus also did on the night of his betrayal when he offered **communion** to his disciples! *The Lords Supper was a sign of Him being linked to the Melchizedek order* of priesthood because he was about to offer his **body** as a sacrifice on the cross and his **blood** as an offering for the sins of mankind!

David is the first to reveal that the **Messiah would be after the order of Melchizedek.** Psalm 110 is considered a Messianic psalm speaking of the messiah to come!

> "The Lord said unto my Lord, ***Sit thou at my right hand, until I make thine enemies thy footstool***. The Lord shall send the rod of thy strength out of Zion: rule thou in the midst of thine enemies. Thy people shall be willing in the day of thy power, in the beauties of holiness from the womb of the morning: thou hast the dew of thy youth. The Lord hath sworn, and will not repent, ***Thou art a priest for ever after the order of Melchizedek.*** The Lord at thy right hand shall strike through kings in the day of his wrath. He shall judge among the heathen, he shall fill the places with the dead bodies; he shall wound the heads over many countries. He shall drink of the brook in the way: therefore shall he lift up the head." Psalm 110:1-7

Notice that he says he is of the Melchizedek order "**forever**". This is not an **earthly priesthood** but a **heavenly priesthood**.
Again, the binary code reveals these **two kinds of priesthoods!**

In the Book of Hebrews Paul explains the function of the h**igh priest**

> "Every ***high priest*** is selected from among the people and is appointed to represent the people in matters related to God, to offer gifts and sacrifices for sins." Heb 5:5 (NIV)

Then he goes on to says that **Jesus is our high priest** in the order of **Melchizedek** giving reference to the Psalm 110 passage above:

> "...You are a ***priest*** forever, in the ***order of Melchizedek***., During the days of Jesus' life on earth, he offered up prayers and petitions with fervent cries and tears to the one who could save him from death, and he was heard because of his reverent submission. Son though he was, he learned obedience from what he suffered and, once made perfect, he became the source of eternal salvation for all who obey him and ***was designated by God to be high priest in the order of Melchizedek***." Hebrews 5:6-10 (NIV)

Let's look again at that passage in in Genesis because it reveals *another*

binary aspect of Melchizedek!

> "And Melchizedek ***king of Salem*** brought forth bread and wine: and he was the ***priest*** of the most high God." Genesis 14"18

Here we see that Melchizedek **was both a King and a Priest**!

The name Melchizedek is the combination of two Hebrew words, the first being ***melek*** meaning **"king"** and the second which is ***tsedeq*** or "righteousness" (Strong's #H4442). So, he is a righteous King. Again, this Messianic term was referred to by Jeremiah and later applied to Jesus:

> "Behold, the days are coming," declares the LORD, "When I will raise up for David a ***righteous*** Branch; And He will ***reign as king*** and act wisely and do justice and ***righteousness*** in the land." Jeremiah 23:5

Now the symbolism is clearer. T**he Melchizedek Priesthood would be an eternal position of both righteous King and high Priest**. It is interesting to note that we see a binary type of this duel ministry when the Jews returned from Babylon. They had Jerusalem and, in all effect, all of Israel run by co-rulers. They set in Zerubbabel as governor (or king) and Joshua as high priest. Zerubbabel was the grandson of King Jeconiah from the Davidic and kingly line of Judah and Joshua was a descendant of Aaron, the priestly line. This co-regency speaks of the shared rule of both Monarchy and Priesthood, a perfect type of Messiah being King and Priest!

Another thing to note is that it says Melchizedek was the king of the city of **Salem**. Salem would later be called Jerusalem, where Messiah would be cut off. But in the eternal city of the **New Jerusalem** Jesus will be King and Priest forever! **Salem means Peace** and Jesus is the **Prince of peace!**

In the new Testament Paul in the book of Hebrews makes reference to Melchizedek:

> "For this ***Melchizedek, king of Salem, priest of the most high God,*** who met Abraham returning from the slaughter of the kings, and blessed him; To whom also Abraham ***gave a tenth part of all;*** first being by interpretation ***King of righteousness***, and after that also King of Salem, which is, ***King of peace!***" Hebrews 7:1,2

Some believe this may have been a Christophany, an appearance of Jesus in the old Testament (like the fourth man in the fiery furnace in Daniel). Paul seems to hint at this when we read the strange qualities of this man Melchizedek!

> "Without father, without mother, without descent, having neither beginning of days, nor end of life; but made like unto the **Son of God**; abideth a priest

continually. Now consider how great this man was, unto whom even the patriarch Abraham gave the tenth of the spoils." Hebrews 7:3,4

It would be considered blasphemy to give tithes to a man, so Abraham no doubt thought this was more than a man, perhaps the promised Messiah! Paul goes on to say:

"For it is evident that ***our Lord*** sprang out of Judah; of which tribe Moses spake nothing concerning priesthood.. And it is yet far more evident: for that ***after the similitude of Melchizedek there ariseth another priest,*** Who is made, not after the law of a carnal commandment, but after the power of an ***endless*** life. For he testifieth, ***Thou art a priest for ever after the order of Melchizedek***" Hebrews 7:14-17

Judah was the royal linage of kingship and Jesus was a descendant of David from the tribe of Judah thus Jesus is the **kingly** Lion of the tribe of Judah! Yet Paul in Hebrews says there is a mystery here because no priests were from the tribe of Judah. They were from the tribe of Levi! The mystery is solved in the fact that Jesus is not of the Levitical priesthood or of the Aaronic order, but Jesus was of the **order of Melchizedek and Gods heavenly High Priest.**

"Where ***Jesus*** has gone as a forerunner on our behalf, having become ***a high priest forever after the order of Melchizedek***." Hebrews 6:20 (ESV)

The Aaronic priesthood ministered to earthly things, but Jesus to heavenly things. Jesus is our **high pries**t who offered his own body as a sacrifice and spilled his blood to cleanse us and present us faultless before the throne of God! He also is the great **intercessor** and **mediator** between God and man!

"Wherefore he is able also to save them to the uttermost that come unto God by him, seeing he ever liveth to make intercession for them.." Hebrews 7:25

"For there is one God, and one mediator between God and men, the man Christ Jesus."1 Timothy 2:5

Chapter 11 - Remembering and Forgetting - the Binary Code of Memory

Memory – Both Good and Bad

Remembering and **forgetting** is a binary act of the mind. It can be **good** or **bad**. Sometimes it is good to **remember** things and sometimes it is not so good. Sometimes it is good to **forget** things and other times it is bad to forget things. We will see that God even has things he wants us to remember and has things he wants us to forget.

Memory is the ability to recall an event, experience, or thought that you had in the **past**. Certain things **in the past** are good to remember and retain while certain things **in our past** are definitely best to forget! *Both remembering and forgetting* ***always deals with the past!*** Although memory deals with the past it can *have a profound effect on the present, as well as the future.*

Much of what we are taught even from a child is to be retained for use later in life. **Knowledge** and **experience** can serve us well later in life. School education is preparation for life as well as work experience. Even bad things can serve to teach us lessons like overcoming failure, defeat, and adversity. We can often learn much from our mistakes, yet some people never learn!

Forgetting the Past

Personally, I think forgetfulness is a part of the curse, but because of our sin nature, perhaps at times it is a blessing. Forgetting can be inadvertent (such as in senility) or purposeful when we choose to forget or deny and suppress the past! And more often than not we probably can be accused of selective memory which is remembering only what we want to!

Remembering the Past

One of the great sayings is that **"Those who do not learn from history are doomed to repeat it!"** What this says is often we forget what happened in the past and rather than learning our lesson we fall back into the same trap! God knew man has the tendency to forget. In the old testament God created Jewish feasts for the purpose of putting Israel in **remembrance** of Gods work in their lives.

God often used **signs** as a means of remembrance. After the **Flood** he put the **rainbow** in the sky when it rained to remind the people that He promised not to destroy the earth again by water!

After the **exodus**, God had to constantly remind the children of Israel how **He delivered and provided for them in the wilderness** and yet they constantly complained and murmured against him.

After they entered **the promised land,** He had to constantly remind them through Joshua that as God did miracles and provided for them in the wilderness so could he deliver them and enable them to conquer the promised land! So quickly they forgot the parting of the sea and the drowning of the armies of Pharaoh. David through the Spirit even declared this in the psalms.

> "Some trust in chariots, and some in horses: but we will ***remember*** the name of the LORD our God." Psalm 20:7

David spoke often of his sinful past in the Psalms but also prayed that God would forget the sins of his youth and called on his mercy! (Psalm 25:7, Psalm.79:8)

Later God would send **prophets** to Israel to remind them of God's faithfulness in the past, as well as to prophecy and warn them of the future!

> "***Remember*** this and shew yourselves men: bring it again to mind, O ye transgressors. ***Remember*** the former things of old: for I am God, and there is none else; I am God, and there is none like me, ***Declaring the end from the beginning,*** and ***from ancient times the things that are not yet done,*** saying, My counsel shall stand, and I will do all my pleasure." Isaiah 46: 8-10

God sent the prophets to get them to remember their rebellious ways to bring them to repentance!!

"Then shall ye ***remember your own evil ways***, and your doings that were not good, and shall loathe yourselves in your own sight for your iniquities and for your abominations." Ezekiel 36:31

Jewish fathers were taught in the scripture to **teach the children** the history of their past so that every generation would remember the great work of God!

"***Remember*** today that your children were not the ones who saw and experienced the discipline of the LORD your God: his majesty, his mighty hand, his outstretched arm... ***teach them to your children, talking about them when you sit at home and when you walk along the road, when you lie down and when you get up. Write them on the door frames of your houses and on your gates,*** so that your days and the days of your children may be many in the land the LORD swore to give your ancestors, as many as the days that the heavens are above the earth." Deuteronomy 11:2, 19-21 (NIV)

Jewish Memorials

The Feast of **Passover** is a feast to **remember** that God through Moses delivered them from Egypt!

"Do not eat it with bread made with yeast, but for seven days eat unleavened bread, the bread of affliction, because you left Egypt in haste—so that all the days of your life you may ***remember*** the time of your departure from Egypt." Deuteronomy 16:3 (NIV)

During **Sukkot** or the **Feast of Tabernacles** Jews erect booths and hang fruit on it to remember God providing for them as they dwelt in tents in the wilderness!

Yom Kippur or the **Day of Atonement** was to be a **day of remembrance**. The High priest would offer up a sacrifice for the year, so it was a time of fasting and a time to enumerate one's misdeeds and contemplate one's faults.

Even the **Sabbath** is a remembrance of God resting on the seventh day and a reminder that we too are to rest from our labors and enjoy the fruits of our labor! It was so important, he carved it into stone on the tablet of the Ten Commandments!

"***Remember*** the ***sabbath day***, to ***keep it holy***. Six days shalt thou labor, and do all thy work: But the seventh day is the sabbath of the LORD thy God: in it thou shalt not do any work, thou, nor thy son, nor thy daughter, thy manservant, nor thy maidservant, nor thy cattle, nor thy stranger that is within thy gates: For in six days the LORD made heaven and earth, the sea, and all that in them is, and rested the seventh day: wherefore the ***LORD blessed the sabbath day, and hallowed it.*** " Exodus 20:8

It is the only commandment where God specifically tells us to remember! Perhaps that is the one we tend to forget! These feasts and events were called **memorials**, meaning **times to remember!**

Jesus also had to often remind his own disciples of things he had previously said and done. One time when He told them to beware of the leaven of the Pharisees, they completely missed the point and thought he was talking about bread. They had already forgotten how he had multiplied the fish and loaves!

"And when Jesus knew it, he saith unto them, Why reason ye, because ye have no bread? ***perceive ye not yet, neither understand***? have ye your heart yet hardened? Having eyes, see ye not? and having ears, hear ye not? and ***do ye not remember***?" Mark 8:18

Jesus warned the disciples of events in the future and instructed them to **remember** His words when they happened!

"They shall put you out of the synagogues: yea, the time cometh, that whosoever killeth you will think that he doeth God service. And these things will they do unto you, because they have not known the Father, nor me. ***But these things have I told you, that when the time shall come, ye may remember that I told you of them.*** And these things I said not unto you at the beginning, because I was with you." John 16:2-4

Releasing and Embracing

'Brethren, I count not myself to have apprehended: but this one thing I do, ***forgetting those things which are behind***, and reaching forth unto t***hose things which are before***, I press toward the mark for the prize of the high calling of God in Christ Jesus." Phil 3:13,14

Paul says that there are some things that we must let go of, release, and forget while there are other things before us that we must reach for and embrace. We must let go of our sinful **past** and embrace a new **future**!

"Therefore, if any man be in Christ, he is a new creature: ***old things are passed*** away; behold, all things are become ***new***." Philippians 2:13

We all go through **seasons** in our life where we must **embrace or**

release things. These are the **binary experiences** we all share, and those experiences all have their **purpose**. Look at this amazing **binary list of dual purposes** in the book of Ecclesiastes:

> "To everything there is a ***season***,
> and a time to every ***purpose*** under the heaven:
>
> A time to be ***born***, and a time to ***die***;
> a time to ***plant***, and a time to ***pluck up*** that which is planted;
> A time to ***kill***, and a time to ***heal***;
> a time to ***break down***, and a time to ***build up***;
> A time to ***weep***, and a time to ***laugh***;
> a time to ***mourn***, and a time to ***dance***;
> A time to ***cast away stones***, and a time to ***gather stones*** together;
> a time to ***embrace***, and a time to ***refrain from embracing;***
> A time to ***get***, and a time to ***lose***;
> a time to ***keep***, and a time to ***cast away***;
> A time to ***rend***, and a time to ***sew***;
> a time to ***keep silence***, and a time to ***speak***;
> A time to ***love***, and a time to ***hate***;
> a time of ***war***, and a time of ***peace***." Ecclesiastes 3:1-8

We will go through times that are complete **opposite** of each other and experience things **good** as well as **bad,** but we can learn from both and if we derive its meanings and purposes, it will help us to grow as individuals! Unfortunately, in life we do not just receive the **knowledge** of good and evil, but the **experience** of good and evil, yet the bible says there is purpose in it all.

> "And we know that all things work together for good to them that love God, to them who are the called according to his ***purpose***." Romans 8:28

The main purpose is to give thanks to God and trust that he is always in control of our lives!

> "In everything **give thanks**: for this is the will of God in Christ Jesus concerning you." 1 Thessalonians 5:18

God Forgets

Forgiving and forgetting is something we must choose to do. Many often say they forgive but can't forget. Because God is God, he cannot forget anything, yet he has said that He **chooses** to forgive and forget our sins.

"I will forgive their wickedness and will ***remember their sins no more***" (Jeremiah 31:34).

How awesome is it that God is so gracious to not only cleanse us of our sinful past but to blot them out from His memory when we truly turn to Him and away from our sinful past!

"I am he who ***blots*** out your transgressions for my own sake, and I ***will not remember*** your sins. "Isaiah 43:25 (NIV)

Remember east and west mean eternal and everlasting:

"As far as the ***east is from the west***, so far has He removed our transgressions from us." Psalm 103:12 (NIV)

He has even said he will **hide** our sins in the **depth of the seas**.

"He will turn again; he will have compassion upon us; he will subdue our iniquities; and thou wilt ***cast all their sins into the depths of the sea.***" Mic.7:19

If God has forgiven us, then **we must forgive ourselves.** The devil wants to constantly remind you of them, but we must forget the past and remember God's grace and look to an eternal future with Him in the kingdom of God!

We must forget when we are to forget and remember when we need to remember. The Bible says that God has a **Book of Remembrance** (*Malachi 3:16–18, (Exodus 32:32*)! Many will be judged by that book and give account of their actions! Hopefully, it has a list of the good we have done and has blotted out the bad!

Chapter 12 - The Two Adams - the Binary Code of Redemption

Sin vs Salvation

Paul, in talking about the resurrected body, unveiled an interesting revelation of the type and anti-type of the **two Adams.**

> "It is sown a ***natural body***; it is raised a ***spiritual body.*** There is a natural body, and there is a spiritual body. And so it is written, "The ***first man Adam*** became ***a living being***." ***The last Adam*** became a ***life-giving spirit***." 1 Corinthians 15:44,45 (NKJV)

Jesus was called **the second Adam** because just as Adam brought forth a linage of his own kind to populate the **earth,** so Christ would begin to populate **heaven** with a race of redeemed and ultimately resurrected men! **Adam brought forth man in his likeness** and **Christ brings forth men after His likeness**! The first Adam went forth and **replenished the earth** and the Second is **replenishing the heavens**! Because of Adam's sin the entrance to the Garden was barred. Prior to Christs resurrection the entrance to heaven was barred. The first Adam was a **living being** created by God in the first days! The last Adam is a **life-giving Spirit** that will resurrect life in the last days!

Through the First Adam sin entered the world and passed on to all mankind.

> "Wherefore, as by ***one man sin entered into the world, and death*** by sin; and so death ***passed upon all men***, for that all have sinned." Romans 5:12

Through the **Second Adam** Salvation was obtained through Christ and offered to all mankind!

> "***Salvation*** is found in no one else, for there is ***no other name*** under heaven given to mankind by which we must be saved." Acts 4:12 (NIV)

The first Adam introduced sin because of the **act of disobedience**. Jesus brought forth forgiveness of sin through the **act of obedience**.

"For if by ***one man's offense*** death reigned by one; much more they which receive abundance of grace and of the ***gift of righteousness*** shall reign in life by one, ***Jesus Christ***.) Therefore as by the ***offense*** of one judgment came upon all men to condemnation; even so by the ***righteousness*** of one the free gift came upon all men unto justification of life. For as ***by one man's disobedience many were made sinners,*** so ***by the obedience of one shall many be made righteous***. Moreover the law entered, that the offense might abound. But where sin abounded, grace did much more abound: That as ***sin*** hath reigned unto death, even so might ***grace*** reign through righteousness unto eternal life by Jesus Christ our Lord." Romans 5:17-21

Jesus said he always did what the Father asked of Him (John 4:34), but his obedience was not just to the will of the Father but to the purpose of the incarnation. Jesus had to be obedient to the purpose of sacrificing his life for the lives of all humanity. He had to be obedient unto death!

"And being found in appearance as a man, he humbled himself by becoming ***obedient to death***- even death on a cross!" Philippians 2:8 (NIV)

The Two Bodies

The contrasts are huge, yet the symbolism of the type is clear. Adam was the first created man with a **physical body** Jesus was the first man with a resurrected **spiritual body.** The first Adam was **earthly,** but the Second Adam is **heavenly**:

"The spiritual did not come first, but the ***natural***, and after that the ***spiritual***. The first man was of the dust of the ***earth***; the second man is of ***heaven***. As was the earthly man, so are those who are of the earth; and as is the ***heavenly man,*** so also are those who are of heaven. And just as we have borne the image of the ***earthly man***, so shall we bear the image of the heavenly man." 1 Corinthians 15:46-49 (NIV)

The physical body of man has great limitations set upon it. It is not only limited to the physical realm, but it even has great limitations within that realm. We can only see so far. We can only hear so much. There are animals that can see and hear better than us. We are confined and limited to time, space, and matter.

When Jesus rose from the dead, he received the first **resurrected and transformed body**. He entered the upper room when the door was locked.

He could simply walk through those walls or transport himself from place to place. Angels seem to have the ability to move in and out of the physical realm. They appeared in Peter's jail cell and though they had spiritual bodies, they could interact with the physical realm. One of the angels kicked Peter to wake him up and then he opened up the jail cell doors to let him out. When Paul and Silas were worshiping in jail, there too the doors were opened and their chains fell off.

Our bodies use our five senses to communicate with the physical realm around us. But there is also a spiritual dimension with angels and demons that we can't interact with apart from God's Spirit (or Satanic influence). The Holy Spirit can bring the human spirit into that realm at times. He did this with many prophets that often saw things in other places **by the Spirit** or were transported to other places **in the Spirit.** The Holy Spirit works in a higher dimension and thus can manipulate the physical realm. The Holy Spirit physically transported Phillip from one town to another.

> "So he commanded the chariot to stand still. And both Philip and the eunuch went down into the water, and he baptized him. Now when they came up out of the water, ***the Spirit of the Lord caught Philip away, so that the eunuch saw him no more;*** and he went on his way rejoicing. But ***Philip was found at Azotus***. And passing through, he preached in all the cities till he came to Caesarea." Acts 8:38-40

Ezekiel was a captive in **Babylon** but was transported in the Spirit several times to **Jerusalem** (Eze. 8:3, 11:14, 43:5). Paul was transported to heaven but could not tell if he was in the spirit or in his body (2 Cor. 12:2). **Elijah** evidently was often transported physically by the Holy Spirit. After he was taken up in the fiery chariot before Elisha, fifty prophets insisted on searching for him, because they said often he was taken up by the spirit, and transported to some mountain top (2 Kings 2:16-18 see also 1 Kings 18:11-12).

Jesus after his resurrection often appeared and disappeared in a physical body such as on the road to Emmaus. Perhaps these things are a foreshadow of the ability of the spiritual resurrected body we shall have through the work of the second Adam!

The Seed and the Tree

The first Adam came forth from the ground with **a natural body** but Jesus, the second Adam resurrected from the earth with a **Spiritual Body.** His death was like a seed that would produce a new form from the ground!

> "But someone will ask, "How are the dead raised? With ***what kind of body*** will they come?" How foolish! What you sow does not come to life unless it dies. When you sow, ***you do not plant the body that will be, but just a seed,*** perhaps of wheat or of something else. But God gives it a body as he has determined, and to ***each kind of seed he gives its own body.*** " 1 Corinthians 15:35-38 (NIV)

In these passages Paul is talking about sowing seed. He says that the body of the seed that is planted into the ground is different than the body of the plant that comes out of the ground. The analogy here is that just as the **plant** is so different from the **seed,** the **resurrected body** is entirely different than the **physical body.**

Jesus makes this same contrast with his parable of the mustard seed and the Kingdom of God:

> "Another parable put he forth unto them, saying, ***The kingdom of heaven*** is like to a ***grain of mustard seed***, which a man took, and sowed in his field: Which indeed is the least of all seeds: but ***when it is grown, it is the greatest among herbs, and becometh a tree***, so that the birds of the air come and lodge in the branches thereof." Matthew . 13:31-32

The difference between a **seed** and a **tree** is huge. Jesus was the seed planted into the earth and out of his resurrection a tree of his kingdom has grown over the millennial to bring many into the kingdom of God. This is the difference between the physical realm and the spiritual realm; the earthly and the heavenly. The ways of man and the ways of God.:

> "For as the heavens are ***higher*** than the earth, so are my ways ***higher*** than your ways, and my thoughts than your thoughts." Isaiah 55:9

The point here, is the huge difference between the work of the first Adam and the second Adam. Adam is head of the old creation corrupted by sin. Jesus is head of the new creation made righteous by grace! Adam brought forth death upon the whole of mankind, but Jesus brought forth Life for those who believe. This eternal life will culminate in the resurrection of the believers.

> "For as in Adam all die, even so in Christ shall all be made alive."
> 1 Corinthians 15:22

So here we see the dual binary Adams and the differences:

1. **Two Men:** The First Adam and the Second Adam (Christ)

2. **Two Acts:** Adam disobeys God and eats the fruit in the Garden and

brings sin upon the whole of humanity! Christ obeys God and goes to the cross to bring salvation to all of mankind!

3. Two Results: The first Adam: sin, condemnation, judgment, and death. The Second Adam: forgiveness, righteousness, grace, and eternal life.

Son of Man and Son of God

Jesus was called **the Son of man** at times and **the Son of God**. That is because though he was a part of the godhead, He chose to be born of man to redeem man. **Son of man was an idiom for Son of Adam**. Jesus is referred to as the "Son of Man" eighty-eight times in the New Testament. When Jesus was incarnated, he was the seed of a woman and the impartation of the Holy Spirit. He did not have an earthly father less he became corrupted by the effects of sin. God chose instead that through a virgin, He would supernaturally create a human form, that would be subject to the physical realm but not subject to the corruption of Adams genetic curse. Jesus had the same limitations in his body as us. He was hungry and ate, he got tired and slept, but Jesus also could draw from the power of the Holy Spirit and do creative miracles and heal. He was both the **Son of Man** and the **Son of God** and unlike any individual that has dwelt on the earth before.

Whereas the **first Adam** was a combination of dust and the breath of God, the **Second Adam** was a unique combination of physical body without the sin nature and the divine essence of the Godhead dwelling within him!

> "And ***the Word*** became ***flesh*** and dwelt among us, and we have seen his glory, glory as of the only Son from the Father, full of grace and truth". 1 John 1:14

Dual Meaning of Son of Man

Even the term "Son of Man" has a binary code that the scribes and religious leaders did not pick up on in Jesus day! Though the term can often be used for man (Psalm 8:4), it is usually a **Messianic title** and the Rabbis have always referenced this title to the Messiah! The term "Son of Man" is actually translated as "Messiah" in the Targum (an Aramaic translation of the Old Testament). That is because the term **Son of man** was used in the old testament as a foreshadow of Christ (Messiah) and his kingdom. Daniel spoke about the Son of Man (messiah) who would have an **eternal kingdom**, therefore making him more than a man:

> "I was watching in the night visions, and behold, one like the ***son of man,*** coming with the clouds of heaven! He came to the ancient of days, and they brought him near before him. Then to him was given dominion and glory and ***a kingdom,*** that all peoples, nations, and languages should serve him. His dominion is ***an everlasting dominion***, which shall not pass away, and his kingdom the one which **shall** not be destroyed." Dan. 7:13,14 (NKJV)

The Book of Enoch although not canonical was often read in the early church and uses the term "Son of Man" as a title for a preexisting divine being who would be revealed in the end days as the judge of men!

The term "Son of Man" was often used by rabbis to refer to Messiah! This is why the Jews were so furious with Stephen because he publicly declared that Jesus was the Messiah whom they had crucified! It was when Stephen called him the **Son of Man** they got enraged and stoned him:

> "But he, being full of the Holy Ghost, looked up stedfastly into heaven, and saw the glory of God, and Jesus standing on the right hand of God, And said, Behold, I see the heavens opened, and the ***Son of man*** standing on the right hand of God. Then they cried out with a loud voice, and stopped their ears, and ran upon him with one accord, And cast him out of the city, and ***stoned him***." Acts 7:55-58

This event was prophesied by Jesus and Stephen was privileged to witness it! Three times Jesus declared that he would again sit at the right hand of God (Mark 14:62, Matthew 26:64, Luke 22:69.)

This messianic term "Son of Man" was often boldly used by Jesus in **reference to himself**: He even asked his disciples:

> "Who do men say the ***Son of man*** is?" Matthew 16:13

Because it is also a reference to man in the old testament the Jews did not think **Jesus was calling himself Messiah** but indeed, he was. This is more than just a statement that he was a man, because when we look at the **context** of the references, He clearly was referring to himself as the Messiah! In these passages Jesus declares that the "Son of Man":

- Is Lord of the Sabbath (Matthew 12:8)
- Shall return with the Angels (Matthew 13:41)
- Came to save those who are lost (Matthew 18:11)

- Has power to forgive sin (Mark 2:10)
- Would suffer, be rejected, killed, and be raised the third day. (Luke 9:22)
- Has authority to execute judgment (John 5:27)
- Will sit at the right hand of God and come again in the clouds. (Mark 14:62)

When Jesus referred to himself as the **Son of Man**, he was declaring that he indeed was the promised **Messiah**, but the ears of the Jews were closed to this open declaration! For hundreds of years they were waiting on the deliverer but when he came, even when He openly declaring himself as the Messiah, they refused to believe.

The Two Brides of the Two Adams

When God put Adam in the Garden of Eden, he made a **wife in Adam's likeness** and brought her to him to be his bride. She would share in his domain and rule with him on the earth. God also made a **Bride for the second Adam.** He established **the church** in Christ's likeness to be the **Bride of Christ:**

> "Let us rejoice and exult and give him the glory, for the ***marriage of the Lamb*** has come, and ***his Bride*** has made herself ready; it was granted her to clothe herself with fine linen, bright and pure"— for the fine linen is the righteous deeds of the saints. And the angel said to me, "Write this: Blessed are those who are invited to the ***marriage supper of the Lamb.***" And he said to me, "These are the true words of God." Revelation 18:7-9 (ESV)

This mystery of the marriage and the first union of Adam and Eve was that it was to be a type of the relationship between the Second Adam and the Church, that is the redeemer and the redeemed:

> "For this cause shall a man leave his father and mother, and shall be joined unto his wife, and they two shall be one flesh. This is a great mystery: but I speak concerning ***Christ and the church.***" Ephesians 5:31

In marriage it is said that a woman and man become one flesh or one body. This is why the church in scripture is called **the Body of Christ**. In marriage, there is a **physical union**. In Christ there is a **spiritual union.** Marriage is a type of this intimate union of Christ and his people. A man and woman now can live together. Jesus uses the word "abide" to express this union which means" to live and dwell with".

"If you abide in me and I abide in you..." John 15:4

Adam and Eve and the symbolism of marriage is a fitting type of Christ and **his love for the church.**

"Husbands, ***love your wives***, as ***Christ loved the church*** and gave himself up for her, that he might sanctify her, having cleansed her by the washing of water with the word, so that he might present the church to himself in splendor, without spot or wrinkle or any such thing, that she might be holy and without blemish." Ephesians 5:25-27 (ESV)

When Gods people are gathered in heaven the celebration is likened to a marriage feast.

"And the angel said to me, "Write this: Blessed are those who are invited to the ***marriage supper of the Lamb***." And he said to me, "These are the true words of God." Revelation 19:9 (NIV

So clearly, the binary brides from the beginning, show the ultimate purpose of a loving relationship between man and his Maker, and not just an impersonal recognition of the Creator by his creation. Jesus came to show the heart of God to mankind. God is not just a faraway deistic deity that is not involved with his creation, but rather seeks to redeem and restore man back to Himself, by the single sacrifice of love. The bible says, "God is love!" (1 John 4:8) and Jesus is the express image of God (Heb.1:3) and therefore contrary to Satan and his demons and evil men who chose to **hate** we must walk in the **love** of God!

Chapter 13 - The Lamb and the Lion - the Binary Code of Messiah

The Two Natures

"So I wept much, because no one was found worthy to open and read the scroll, or to look at it. But one of the elders said to me, "Do not weep. Behold, the ***Lion of the tribe of Judah***, the Root of David, has prevailed to open the scroll and to loose its seven seals. And I looked, and behold, in the midst of the throne and of the four living creatures, and in the midst of the elders, stood ***a Lamb*** as though it had been slain, having seven horns and seven eyes, which are the seven Spirits of God sent out into all the earth. Then He came and took the scroll out of the right hand of Him who sat on the throne." Revelation 5:4-7 (NKJV)

In this passage John in his vision on the Isle of Patmos weeps because no one is worthy to open the scroll and an elder tells him the **Lion of the Tribe if Judah** is worthy, but when he turns to see him he sees a **Lamb** instead of a Lion! Why do we have to see the Lamb before we can see the Lion?

This is the mystery of the **Binary Code of the Jewish Messiah**. The messianic scriptures in the old testament reveal a **dual nature of Messiah.** Some scriptures point to him as having a humble, gentle, and sacrificial nature and other scriptures point to him as being strong, mighty, bold and conquering! In the old testament there are both Lion references to messiah and Lamb references. The Jews at the time of Christ were under the occupation of the Roman empire, and naturally were looking for Messiah to come as the great deliverer, so they gravitated to the Lion nature in scriptures, and failed to see Jesus because he displayed the Lamb nature!.

The Two Comings!

Another thing hid from the nation of Israel was that there were actually two comings of Messiah. The first time he would come as a **Lamb** and the second time as a **Lion**! These clearly explains the different Messianic texts and this is why there are two comings of Christ. He came as a **sacrificial Lamb** the first time and is coming in the second coming as a **conquering Lion**. The reason why it was hidden from the Jews is so that he could bring the gentiles into the Kingdom. When the "Times of the Gentiles" is over, he will take out his Church, and then open Israel's eyes again so that He might restore them to himself!

> "For I would not, brethren, that ye should be ignorant of this ***mystery***, lest ye should be wise in your own conceits; that blindness in part is happened to Israel, until the ***fullness of the Gentiles*** be come in." Romans 11:25

The Jews rejected and crucified Jesus and just as Jesus predicted, within a generation Titus came in and destroyed the city of Jerusalem as well as the temple. The Jews were scattered to all the nations as their prophets had foretold. This was so that the gospel message could go out into all the world and not merely be contained to one nation.

> "They will fall by the edge of the sword and be led captive among all nations, and Jerusalem will be trampled underfoot by the Gentiles, until the ***times of the Gentiles are fulfilled.***" Luke 21:24 (ESV)

At the end of the ages, Jesus will return as the conquering Lion of Judah and judge the whole earth!

The First Coming- The Lamb of God!

The Jews should have gotten their first hint from the forerunner of Messiah. When John the Baptist was baptizing in the wilderness, he revealed who Jesus was when he first saw him:

"The next day John seeth Jesus coming unto him, and saith, Behold the ***Lamb of God***, which taketh away the sin of the world." John 1:29

In Judaic terms most Jews understood the purpose and symbolism of a lamb. Lambs were slaughtered and offered up as a sacrifice for sins. Daily the people brought lambs to the priests to offer up as a sacrifice for their sins. John the Baptist stated this purpose when he said, "...***who takes away the sins of the world***". The first coming of Messiah was to die for mankind.

One of the well-known messianic scriptures was Isaiah 53.

"...He hath no form nor comeliness; and when we shall see him, there is no beauty that we should desire him. He is despised and rejected of men; a man of sorrows and acquainted with grief: and we hid as it were our faces from him; he was despised, and we esteemed him not. Surely, he hath borne our griefs, and carried our sorrows: yet we did esteem him stricken, smitten of God, and afflicted. But he was ***wounded for our transgressions, he was bruised for our iniquities: the chastisement of our peace was upon him; and with his stripes we are healed.*** All we like sheep have gone astray; we have turned everyone to his own way; and the Lord hath laid on him the iniquity of us all. He was oppressed, and he was afflicted, yet he opened not his mouth: he is ***brought as a lamb to the slaughter***, and as a sheep before her shearers is dumb, so he openeth not his mouth. He was ***taken from prison and from judgment:*** and who shall declare his generation? for he was ***cut off out of the land of the living: for the transgression of my people was he stricken. And he made his grave with the wicked, and with the rich in his death***; because he had done no violence, neither was any deceit in his mouth. Yet it pleased the Lord to bruise him; he hath put him to grief: when thou shalt ***make his soul an offering for sin***, he shall see his seed, he shall prolong his days, and the pleasure of the Lord shall prosper in his hand. He shall see of the travail of his soul and shall be satisfied: by his knowledge shall my righteous servant justify many; for he shall bear their iniquities. Therefore will I divide him a portion with the great, and he shall divide the spoil with the strong; because he hath poured out his soul unto death: and he was numbered with the transgressors; and he bare the sin of many, and made intercession for the transgressors." Isaiah 53:2-12

We see clearly in these passages, that the Messiah is described as a **lamb** led to the slaughter, who was rejected, beaten, bruised, and wounded for our transgressions and would die for the sins of others.

This is exactly what Jesus did on the cross.

The Apostle John in the book of Revelation, saw a mighty angel ask the question who was worthy to open the scroll. In that same chapter it answers that question:

> "In a loud voice they were saying: "***Worthy is the Lamb, who was slain,*** to receive power and wealth and wisdom and strength and honor and glory and praise!" Then I heard every creature in heaven and on earth and under the earth and on the sea, and all that is in them, saying: "***To him who sits on the throne and to the Lamb*** be praise and honor and glory and power, for ever and ever!" The four living creatures said, "Amen," and the elders fell down and worshiped." Revelation 5:12-14 (NIV)

The angels and the elders see Jesus sitting at the right hand of God and recognize him as the **Lamb of God** who takes away the sins of the world!

The lamb's blood was shed on the temple's altar to cover the sins of the people, but they could not see that Jesus was offering his own blood to wash away the sins of man!

God prepared a body, the first Adam in the Garden to establish mankind but he prepared another body (the second Adam) before the foundations of the earth to be offered up as a sacrifice to redeem fallen man. God knew that Adam would sin and so had a **backup plan** that he made even before he made man. *His **contingency plan** was to send His Son into the world to die for the sins of mankind.*

> "Forasmuch as ye know that ye were not ***redeemed*** with corruptible things, as silver and gold, from your vain conversation received by tradition from your fathers; But with ***the precious blood of Christ,*** as of ***a lamb without blemish*** and without spot: Who verily was ***foreordained before the foundation of the world, but was manifest in these last times for you.*** " 1 Peter 1:18-20

The Essenes

The Pharisees and Sadducees could not see the Messiah as the Lamb because of the Lion messianic passages, But there was a third sect of the priesthood called **the Essenes**, who did believe in a Suffering Servant and wrote about it in the Dead Sea Scrolls. John the Baptist is believed to be of this sect and many of their beliefs were strongly Messianic and surprisingly **similar to the beliefs of Christianity.** They thought the priesthood in Jerusalem had become corrupt and thus withdrew to a monastic life in the deserts near the Dead sea! Josephus said they held great affection for each other and had witnessed them preforming exorcisms. They did not believe in animal sacrifice, nor did they own slaves. They believed in water baptism and purification by using mikvehs or ritual baths. They also believed in a **new**

covenant based on Jeremiah and Ezekiel (Jeremiah 31:31-34, Ezekiel 36:24-28)

They were waiting on the Messiah, and even had a type of **communion meal with bread and wine.** They declared that when the messiah did come, he would bless the bread and wine which Jesus did at the Lord's supper." Because **the Essenes suddenly disappeared during the first century**, *many scholars believe that most became Christians and assimilated into the early church.*

The Second Coming- The Lion of Judah!

When the disciples watched Jesus ascend into heaven after his resurrection from **the mount of Olives,** two angels told them he would return in like manner.

> "And when he had spoken these things, while they beheld, he was ***taken up***; and a cloud received him out of their sight. And while they looked stedfastly ***toward heaven*** as he went up, behold, ***two men stood by them in white apparel***; Which also said, Ye men of Galilee, why stand ye gazing up into heaven? ***this same Jesus, which is taken up from you into heaven, shall so come in like manner as ye have seen him go into heaven.*** " Acts 1:9-11

Jesus ascended and was taken up into the heavens and he will one day descend from the heavens and come back to that very same spot on the Mount of Olives.

> "Then the ***LORD*** will go out to fight against those nations, as He ***fights*** in the day of battle. 4On that day His feet will stand on the ***Mount of Olives***, east o Jerusalem..." Zechariah 14:3,4 (NIV)

When he returns, he will not be the timid **lamb** that held his speech before his captors but rather he will be the mighty and bold Lion of Judah who will roar and fight against his enemies. Being of the tribe of Judah means he will fulfill the *messianic qualification of being a descendant of David who was from the tribe of Judah.*

> "And there shall come forth a rod out of the ***stem of Jesse***, and a ***Branch*** shall grow out of his ***roots***: And the ***spirit of the Lord shall rest upon him***, the

spirit of wisdom and understanding, the spirit of counsel and might, the spirit of knowledge and of the fear of the Lord; And shall make him of quick understanding in the fear of the Lord: and he shall not ***judge*** after the sight of his eyes, neither reprove after the hearing of his ears: But with righteousness shall he ***judge*** the poor, and reprove with equity for the meek of the earth: and he shall smite the earth: with the ***rod of his mouth,*** and with the breath of his lips shall he slay the wicked. And righteousness shall be the girdle of his loins, and faithfulness the girdle of his reins...And in that day there shall be ***a root of Jesse***, which shall stand for an ensign of the people; to it shall the Gentiles seek: and his rest shall be glorious" Isaiah 11:1-5,10

Jesse was the father of David and the Jews knew Messiah had to be his descendant. Mary, his natural mother and Joseph, the legal father of Jesus, were **both descendants of David**. That is why they went to Bethlehem when she was pregnant. During the census, the father was required to return to the city he was born in and the Bible calls Bethlehem the city of David.

"And Joseph also went up from Galilee, out of the city of Nazareth, into Judaea, unto the ***city of David,*** which is called ***Bethlehem***; (***because he was of the house and lineage of David***)" Luke 2:4

The genealogies in Mathew one and Luke 3 both confirm that Jesus was a descendant of Judah and thus rightly called the Lion of the tribe of Judah!

The Kingly Tribe

"***Judah*** is a lion's whelp; From the prey, my son, you have gone up. He couches, he lies down as a lion, And as a lion, who dares rouse him up? "***The scepter shall not depart from Judah***, Nor the ruler's staff from between his feet, ***Until Shiloh comes***, And to him shall be the obedience of the peoples." Genesis 49:10 (NAS)

The scepter is the signet and seal of a King. As **Levite is the priestly tribe** so **Judah was the Kingly tribe**. A foreshadow of His kingship and second coming is in John:

"The next day the great crowd that had come for the festival heard that Jesus was on his way to Jerusalem. They took palm branches and went out to meet him, shouting, "Hosanna!" "Blessed is he who comes in the name of the Lord!"

> Blessed is the ***king of Israel!***" Jesus found a young donkey and sat on it, as it is written: "Do not be afraid, Daughter Zion; see, ***your king is coming***, seated ***on a donkey's colt***." At first his disciples did not understand all this. Only after Jesus was glorified did they realize that these things had been written about him and that these things had been done to him." John 12:12-16 (NIV)

As Jesus entered Jerusalem the people cried "Hosanna" and declared him "King of Israel. His riding on the donkey was a fulfillment of a prophecy by Zechariah:

> "Rejoice greatly, Daughter Zion! Shout, Daughter Jerusalem! See, **your king comes to you**, righteous and victorious, lowly and **riding on a donkey,** on a colt, the foal of a donkey." Zechariah 9:9 (NIV)

David had his son **Solomon** ride into town on a donkey to declare him as the king that would succeed him! (1 Kings 1:33). Jesus was announcing himself as King and Messiah. The first time he came humbly on a **white donkey** and they declared him "**King of Israel**". But in Revelations it says that when he comes again, he will be riding **a white horse** and have a sash that calls him "**King of kings**", declaring his kingship over **all** the nations! It was the custom that a King rode a **donkey in times of peace** and **a horse in times of war!** He came as the prince of Peace in his first coming but will come as the captain of the hosts of heaven in his second coming, to bring judgment upon the world!

> "Speak, ye that ride on **white asses**, ye that sit in judgment, and walk by the way" (Judges 5:10)

> "And the armies which were in heaven followed him upon ***white horses***, clothed in fine linen, white and clean. And out of his mouth goeth a sharp sword, that with it he should smite the nations: and he shall rule them with a rod of iron: and he treadeth the winepress of the fierceness and wrath of Almighty God. And he hath on his vesture and on his thigh a name written, ***King of Kings***, And Lord Of Lords." Revelation 19:14-16

The second time, when Jesus returns, he will come boldly to **Judge** mankind! He will rule as a king for a thousand years and ultimately judge Satan, the fallen angels and the wicked who refuse his rule!

The Binary code of Messiah shows a two-fold calling with a twofold purpose of the promised deliverer! The contrast of the **two natures of a lamb and the lion** could not be any greater. *One is meek and one is bold, one is silent, and one roars, one is led to the slaughter and one hunts to slaughter his prey! One offers his outer skin to warm man and the other* *tears the flesh of encroaching man.*

Jesus comes first as a sacrificial lamb but comes the second time as a fierce judge of the unrighteous. Messiah means **deliverer** and he delivered the first time through salvation by love and will deliver the second time through righteousness by wrath. He came **quietly** to a corner of the earth the first time and obtained salvation for all mankind and He will come again **not so quietly**! With a shout and a trumpet sound he will appear before the whole world and the whole world will take notice. Many will try to war against him, but it will be as futile as the war in heaven! Who can fight God and win!

Chapter 14 - Worldliness and Holiness- the Binary Code of Influence

Influence and Exposure

It has been said that a boat is supposed to be in the water, but water is not supposed to be in the boat. What we let into our lives will often influence our lives. We are susceptible to our surroundings, and are influenced by our environment, whether it's the nightly news or the weekly prayer meeting! We are taught as adolescents to be careful of peer pressure, yet often fall into the same thing as adults by people on the job, relatives, or questionable acquaintances!

The bible says that we have three forces always trying to influence us to make the wrong choices**: the world, the flesh, and the devil** (1 John 2:16). Or we can allow ourselves to rather be influenced by the other trinity:

> "For there are three that bear record in heaven, ***the Father, the Word, and the Holy Ghost***: and these three are one." 1 John 5:7

This naturally is the Father, Son (the Word) and Holy Spirit! So, the Binary code of influence breaks things down to two things, **godly or ungodly, the right or the wrong; the Word or the world.** The worldly ways are contrary to the ways of God because it is comprised of another **ungodly trinity**:

> "Love not the world, neither the things that are in the world. If any man love the world, the love of the Father is not in him. For all that is in the world, ***the lust of the flesh***, and ***the lust of the eyes***, and ***the pride of life***, is not of the Father, but is of the world. And the world passeth away, and the lust thereof: but he that doeth the will of God abideth forever." 1 John 2:15-17

Temptation always comes in these three forms. Satan used all three of these in the Garden of Eden.

> "And when the woman saw that the tree was ***good for food,*** and that it was ***pleasant to the eyes***, and a tree to be ***desired to make one wise***, she took of the fruit thereof, and did eat, and gave also unto her husband with her; and he did eat." Genesis 3:6

Notice first, it was" ***good for food***". They physically hungered for it. This is the **lust of the flesh**. They saw it was "p***leasant to the eyes***"! The fruit was attractive to the eye. This is the **"Lust of the eyes."** Then she saw it was "**desired to make one wise**". She desired the understanding of good and evil, and to be like God as Satan promised. This is the "**Pride of life**"! As the scripture say" Pride cometh before a fall (Proverbs 16:18) and that is just what happened, they fell!

It is fascinating that when Jesus was tempted by the devil in the wilderness, he was tested three times by the same three things.

> "Then Jesus was led by the Spirit into the wilderness to be ***tempted*** by the devil. After fasting forty days and forty nights, ***he was hungry***. The tempter came to him and said, "If you are the Son of God, tell these ***stones to become bread***." Jesus answered, "It is written: 'Man shall not live on bread alone, but on every word that comes from the mouth of God. Then the devil took him to the holy city and had him stand on the highest point of the temple. "If you are the Son of God," he said, "***throw yourself down***. For it is written:'He will command his angels concerning you, and they will lift you up in their hands, so that you will not strike your foot against a stone.' Jesus answered him, "It is also written: 'Do not put the Lord your God to the test.' Again, the devil took him to a very high mountain and showed him all ***the kingdoms of the world*** and their splendor. "All this ***I will give you***," he said, "if you will bow down and worship me."Jesus said to him, "Away from me, Satan! For it is written: 'Worship the Lord your God, and serve him only.'"Then the devil left him, and angels came and attended him" Matthew 4:1-11 (NIV)

The first temptation was **the lust (or desires) of the flesh.** Jesus had fasted forty days and Satan was tempting Jesus to turn stones into **bread** which he could have easily done but refused! The second temptation was **the Pride of Life**! Satan tempted Jesus into showing off (pride) by **jumping off a cliff** (Life) to show that the angels would protect him. They would of but again He refused. The third temptation was **the lust of the eyes**! Satan showed him **the Kingdoms of the world** and offered to give them to Jesus if He would simply worship him. The devil does own the kingdoms of the world, but Jesus refused to worship him and in all three temptations he countered with a quote from the Word of God! This is the importance of knowing the scriptures.

So, there is a binary contrast between the **kingdoms of this world** and the **kingdom of God**!

The Danger of the World System

We see from the previous scripture that Satan runs the world and is even called in the bible the "Ruler of this World" (John 14:30, John 16:11). The world is not a planet, it is a **system**. The bible is not talking about the earth when it refers to the world but rather it is talking about an ungodly self-centered system that rules the nations and peoples of the world. It is inherently evil because it is run by Satan and demonic forces.

Because the **world's system** is the opposite of **God's system** it is anti-God, Anti-Christ, anti-bible, and anti-Christian. For this reason, it opposes and even hates godliness and holiness. This is why we are to be **in the world** but not **of the world**!

> "If the ***world hates you***, keep in mind that it ***hated me first.*** If you belonged to the world, it would love you as its own. As it is, ***you do not belong to the world***, but ***I have chosen you out of the world.*** That is why the world hates you." John 15:18-19 (NIV)

> "I have given them your word, and the ***world*** has hated them because ***they are not of the world,*** just as I am not ***of the world***. I do not ask that you take them out of the world, but that you keep them from the evil one. They are not ***of the world***, just as I am not ***of the world.***" John 17:14–16 (ESV)

We do not belong to the **world** we belong now to the **kingdom of God!**

> "Jesus answered, ***My kingdom*** is not of this ***world.***" John 18:36

The world system is contrary to the Bible. We can either be influenced to be **godly** by the Bible or to be worldly through the corruption of the world. Both the world and the Bible have opposing transforming powers on people.

> "And be not ***conformed*** to this world: but be ye ***transformed*** by the renewing of your mind, that ye may prove what [is] ***that good, and acceptable, and perfect, will of God***." Romans 12:2

The **world demands conformity,** but t**he bible and the Holy Spirit brings forth transformation**. With the world we must conform to its wicked system, but Gods Word, Spirit and people help to transform us into the **image of Christ!**

It is unfortunate that many Christians love their lives, possessions, and the things of this world! But Jesus says:

"***Love not the world, neither the things that are in the world.*** If any man loves the world, the love of the Father is not in him."1 John 2:15

"Set your ***affection*** on t***hings above***, not on things on the ***earth***." Colossians 3:2

Compromise and Assimilation

The danger of worldliness is that it starts out with **influence**, then turns into **compromise** then ends up with **assimilation**. The goal of the devil is to get Christians to compromise their faith and ultimately, they will be no different than the world!

Earlier we mentioned the Story of Balaam and Balak. Balak the King of Moab could not get Balaam to curse Israel but what Balaam did later to Israel was probably just as bad. He basically told the King of Moab that he could not curse the people of God, but he could tell him how to destroy them. Balaam knew it was God who blessed Israel, and enabled them to be victorious in conquering the promise land, so he told King Balak, all you have to do is send your women over to them and lure them into relationships, and then marriage, and finally the people would start to abandon God and follow the false gods of the Moabites. By the influence of those idolatrous women, Balaam got Israel to compromise their faith, and soon they backslid from God and fell into fornication and idolatry.

Christians are not immune to this tactic. Jesus warns of this same spirit in the Book of Revelation when He speaks to the church in Pergamos:

"But I have a few things ***against thee***, because thou hast there ***them that hold the doctrine of Balaam***, who taught Balak to cast a ***stumbling block*** before the children of Israel, to eat things sacrificed unto idols, and to commit fornication." Revelation 2:14

Jesus was warning this church that there are people trying to lay a stumbling block before them in the church by **influencing** them to **compromise** their faith.

The Northern tribe, under Jeroboam, not only began to engage in idolatry with the golden calves, but ultimately, they were captured by the Assyrians, and carried off to eventually be assimilated with Babylonians, and other heathens. Those Jews that remained in the land, also got **assimilated** with the Gentiles in those surrounding cities and were mixed with the Samaritans. The Jews in Jesus days hated the Samaritans because they were not pure Jews and they did not worship in Jerusalem. The final step of compromise is **assimilation** where you become just like those around you. The danger of Christians compromising with the world is that you can soon find your no different than the world!

The Sanctity of Holiness.

The opposite of **worldliness** is **holiness**. When we think of holiness we think of Jesus or God but surely don't think of man being holy. Yet the bible says Christians are required by God to be holy!

> 'But just as he who called you is holy, so ***be holy in all you do***; for it is written: "***Be holy, because I am holy***." 1 Peter 1:15-16

> "Make every effort to live in peace with everyone and to ***be holy!***" Hebrews 12:14 (NIV)

It is important first of all to understand what holiness is not. Holiness is not perfection. It is not doing everything right all the time because God knows we are human and imperfect. Holiness is not trying to please men with our conduct or conversation, but holiness is seeking to please God alone with a life that is worthy of his good pleasure! Holiness is not divinity, sainthood, or religious piety. Holiness is not a title, though some Popes and priests love to be called by this title. Holiness is primarily the **condition of the inner man** and not the outer man. It is our condition before God and not a position before men! Holiness is not a movement. It is personal character and conduct!

The scriptures tell us a lot about what holiness is:

> "Therefore, since we have these promises, dear friends, let us ***purify ourselves from everything that contaminates body and spirit,*** perfecting ***holiness*** out of reverence for God." 2 Corinthians 7:1 (NIV)

Part of holiness is removing from our lives the things that can defile our spirit and our body. Only by setting aside sexual immorality, the works of the flesh, and spiritual sin, can we become holy and righteous before him whom we serve.

Holiness starts with examining oneself and letting God shine his light into the dark places of our lives!

"Search me, God, and ***know my heart;*** test me and know my anxious thoughts. ***See if there is any offensive way in me*** and lead me in the way everlasting." Psalm 139:23-24 (NIV)

Holiness is a progressive work! Apart from repentance, holiness is not accomplished by self-effort but by the Holy Spirit cleansing us, reaching us, and leading us into a life pleasing to God!

"Therefore, if anyone ***cleanses*** himself from what is dishonorable, he will be a vessel for honorable use, ***set apart as holy***, useful to the master of the house, ready for every good work." 2 Timothy 2:21 (ESV)

Remember **the binary code often includes division or separation**, God told Israel that they must be separated from all the other nations so that they would be holy and sanctified to Him!

"***You are to be holy*** to me because I, the Lord, am holy, and I have ***set you apart from the nations to be my own.***" Leviticus 20:26 (NIV)

Set apart means **separated and consecrated** to him. This is true holiness!

"But you are a chosen race, a royal priesthood, ***a holy nation***, a ***people for his own possession***, that you may proclaim the excellencies of him who called you out of darkness into his marvelous light."1 Peter 2:9 (ESV)

As the world influences worldliness, so does the Word of God impart holiness!

"How can a young person stay on the path of purity? By ***living according to your word.***" Psalm 119:9 (NIV)

God's word is the guidebook for righteous living, and if we allow its influence rather than the worlds, we will mature in growth, and be equipped to serve God in every good work!

"*...how from infancy you have known* **the Holy Scriptures**, *which are able to make you* **wise** *for salvation through faith in Christ Jesus. All* **Scripture** *is God-breathed and is useful for teaching, rebuking, correcting and training in righteousness, so that the servant of God may be thoroughly equipped for every good work." 2 Timothy. 3:15-17(NIV)*

Chapter 15 - Religion vs Relationship – the Code of the Pursuit of God

Outward Reverence vs Inward Revelation!

Christianity is different than all other religions for two reasons.

First, religion is simply man's belief and **reverence** of a Deity, but Christianity is a **revelation** of God himself. The multiple pagan and cultic religions all acknowledge a Creator and are motivated by their own interpretation of who that might be, but in Christianity (as well as Judaism), God has chosen to **reveal** himself to man.

God warned Israel that they should not have any other Gods before him. He declared that idolatry (the worship of false gods) was an abomination. God first revealed himself to **Israel** to declare there was **only one God** in a world that followed polytheism. Then he revealed His Son **Jesus** as the second part of the trinity to the **world** to show that there was **only one way** to God!

> "Neither is there salvation in any other: for there is ***none other name*** under heaven given among men, whereby we must be saved." Acts 4:12

Second, **religion is based upon an outward knowledge of God,** but **Christianity is based upon a personal relationship with God** the Father through God the Son

> "Jesus saith unto him, I am the way, the truth, and the life: ***no man cometh unto the Father, but by me***." John 14:6

> "Whosoever denieth the Son, the same hath not the Father: ***he that acknowledgeth the Son hath the Father also.***" 1 John 2:23

Religion is outward, often ceremonial, liturgical, and self-effacing. Jesus often clashed with the religious rulers of his day.

"Woe unto you, ***scribes and Pharisees, hypocrites!*** for ye are like unto whited sepulchers, which indeed appear ***beautiful outward***, but are within ***full of dead men's bones***, and of all uncleanness." Matthew 23:27

He called them **beautiful on the outside but dead on the inside,** this is an excellent description of religion. It looks good on the outside but is dead on the inside! Many of our Cathedrals and megachurches portray this as well with massive or elaborate outsides but dead religious activity inside.

Two Kinds of Godliness

True Christianity seeks to make the believer godly. Godly simply means to be Godlike, not that we are to be little Gods (that after all was Satan's goal, to be a God) but to reflect his character. Satan wanted to be like God and even tempted Eve with the same deception by saying if they ate of the forbidden fruit, they "would be like God" (Gen.3:5). This is the wrong kind of godliness when people think they are God, and is the greatest deception,

The other form of a false godliness is a godliness that is purely external, a show and a pretense but neither sincere nor real before God. Paul warned about this being prevalent in the last days!

"Having a ***form of godliness***, but ***denying the power*** thereof: from such turn away." 2 Timothy 3:5

Real godliness has the work of His transforming power within us. It is not self-effort or false piety. Jesus confronted this in his own days with the Pharisees and Sadducee.

"As he taught, Jesus said, "Watch out for the teachers of the law. They like to ***walk around in flowing robes*** and be ***greeted with respect in the market-places*** and have the ***most important seats*** in the synagogues and the ***places of honor*** at banquets. They devour widows' houses and for a s***how make lengthy prayers***. These men will be punished most severely." Mark 12:38-40 | NIV

Notice the indicators of false godliness. The long robes speak of the outer appearance so that they may be recognized by men not God. This is **Pride**. Secondly, they seek after the recognition and greetings of the people in the marketplace. This is **Pandering**! Third is they desire the elevated places with the most prestigious seats in the synagogue and places of honor.

(remember Lucifer desires to elevate his throne above God's). This is **Power**! And finally, they rob the people while they make pious lengthy prayers in the synagogue! This is **Pretense**! Outward piety is no substitute for true inner transformation.

Real godliness attained by the believer, is the working of the Holy Spirit to alter and change the heart, and slowly work the nature of Christ-likeness in our lives. It is being conformed to Christ and transformed by the Holy Spirit!

"For those whom He foreknew, He also predestined to become ***conformed to the image of His Son,*** so that He would be the firstborn among many brethren." Romans 8:29

"And we all, with unveiled face, beholding the glory of the Lord, are ***being transformed into the same image from one degree of glory to another.*** For this comes from the Lord..." Corinthians 3:18 (ESV)

Religiosity is not just confined to other religions or sects. It is unfortunately a part of Christianity. Just as there is the real, there will always be the counterfeit! Jesus warned of false shepherds and hirelings who go through the motion but really do not love the sheep as the true shepherd does.

God Seekers or Men Pleasers

True Christianity has its moorings anchored to God's word! It is sincere and seeks only to please God, while religious folks are trying to please men. We now have huge seeker friendly churches that are set up like cafes and clubs and are using every carnal way to seek to please people to get them into the church building, and sadly it is working.

"For am I now ***seeking the approval of man***, or of ***God***? Or am I trying to ***please man***? If I were still trying to please man, I would not be a servant of Christ." Galatians 1:10 (ESV)

"So as to walk in a manner worthy of the Lord, ***fully pleasing to him,*** bearing fruit in every good work and increasing in the knowledge of God." Colossians 1:10 (ESV)

If we seek to please people, the most we will do is reap man's reward, but if we seek to please God, then we will receive Gods reward! Religion seeks to **appease** God, whereas Christianity seeks to **please** God! True Christianity takes after Jesus who only sought to please the Father!

> "I can do nothing on my own. As I hear, I judge, and my judgment is just, because ***I seek not my own will but the will of him who sent me.***" John 5:30 (ESV)

Everything Jesus did was because of His relationship with the Father, and everything we do is because of our relationship with the Son. Christianity is built upon a personal relationship with our Creator, and redeemer. Religion is man's effort to God rather than Gods revelation of himself to us.

Some ask, "Isn't Allah the same as the Christian God?" No! Not at all! Allah is A lie! Jesus pointed man to the only true God, his Father, and he made once and for all a way for man to be reconciled to God. He said it is finished, and on the cross the final work was done to bring man back to God. The resurrection was the proof! He conquered hell and death, and no other revelation was needed! After the bible was complete, there was no need for any false and contradicting supplement such as the Koran! There also was no need for another mediator or prophet to point to another God! Islam came into being nearly 500 years after Christ! The teaching and lifestyle of Mohammad are in direct contrast to the teachings and lifestyle of Jesus. God is Love, and Jesus was called the prince of peace. Allah displays no love, and Mohammad was a man of war. Islam is a counterfeit religion, and Allah is a false God, and God said he would have no other Gods before him. Mohammad was just a man, but Jesus was not just a man, but the Son of God. Mohammad did no miracles, but Jesus healed the lepers, restored sight to the blind and raised people from the dead. Mohammad is still dead and buried but Jesus was raised from the dead, and his grave is empty to this day!

Jesus was also a prophet. He predicted His own death and resurrection, the destruction of the temple, and the end times! I believe he also predicted Mohammad and Allah when he said:

> "I am come in my Father's name, and ye receive me not: ***if another shall come in his own name, him ye will receive.***" John 5:43

Jesus was saying that he was sent by God, and men would reject him, but after him someone would come in their own name, and men would accept them instead. Who else could Jesus be talking about unless he is also referring to the Antichrist! The binary pursuit of God can be broken down to two ways: man's way or God's way; human effort or divine inspiration; religion through a false and outward system or redemption through personal relationship with our Creator!

Chapter 16 - The Beginning and the End - the Binary Code of Time

The Construct of Time

Time was created by God! He placed it in the realm of his creation for man, not for himself. He sits outside of time and is not subject to it. The Bible is the Manufactures Handbook. It is the Creators Guidebook for man. In the first sentence, of the first chapter, of the first book, it is fitting that it starts out with these three words "In the beginning!" (Gen.1:1). <u>This was the beginning of time</u>. It is followed by the words "God created". When God set the backdrop and environment for man he started with **Time,** then Space, then Matter, He placed the heavenly bodies into place because their movements constitute the flowing of time. God in essence, placed a giant clock in the night sky to mark time. This however is not just a clock! It is a **stopwatch**. When man fell into sin and death began, He started the **timer** and now not only was there **a beginning** but there would be **an end**! When death entered the sphere of man, eternity ceased for the physical realm.

God would now show man his timetable. **Genesis is the story of the beginning, and Revelation the story of the end**. And all throughout the rest of God's words, He would hint of the finiteness of the physical realm, and the few short years of man and His creation. Just as there was a beginning, there will be an end. This is **the binary code of time.**

Time – An Allotment of Events between Birth and Death

Time is given to every man. Some people, for whatever reason, are allotted much time on earth. Others are allotted very little. But that allotment is given by God, and the end of that time is at God's **appointment,** not mans. **Birth** is the beginning of man's existence into the physical realm, and **death** is his **appointment to** exit from it!

> "And as it is ***appointed*** unto men ***once to die***, but after this the judgment." Hebrews 9:27

Man's construct of time is measurable by seconds, minutes, hours, days, years, etc. God's is measured by **events** and actions, or s**easons** of **activity** if you will.

> "There is a time for everything, and a ***season*** for ***every activity*** under the heavens: a time to be ***born*** and a time to ***die...***" Ecclesiastes3:1,2 (NIV)

Linear vs Cyclical Time

Man sees time as **Linear**! To him time is a straight line, a timeline that has a simple beginning and an end! God, however, sees time as **cyclical and repeatable**. Time to man is linear like an old record player. You put the needle down at the beginning and if you want to go to a particular song on the record you have to wait until you arrive at that spot. God sees time like a CD player. A CD player can locate any song on it by going directly to that spot. God can at any time go to any event in our lives past, present, and future. We cannot.

However, many of the ***events*** in our lives are usually not just one-time events, but rather repeatable occurrences, or similar experiences so we can learn from them and grow. If we don't learn our lesson from an event, whether pleasant or not, it will come back again. God places us in cyclical situations to teach us, correct us, motivates, and even convict us!

If we look at God's timepiece which are the heavens, we see most everything is cyclical not linear. Things don't just start at one point and end at another. The planets orbit around the sun, and then repeat the cycle. The moon orbits around the earth, and then repeats. Astronomers know that whole solar systems orbit in galaxies, and then repeat the motions. Even comets, though they may not return for thousands of years, follow a cyclical path and repeat.

A clock uses cogs, gears, and levers to repeat cycles in order to measure time. Even a grandfather clock, uses a swinging pendulum in a repeatable pattern, to tick off the passing of time. Why this cyclical pattern? This leads us to the purpose of time!

The Purpose of Time

The allotment of time is what we call life. This is the culmination of all our experiences and events. They often seem random to us, but there is great purpose in them, and many see the hand of providence in much of the events of their lives.

As stated before, we often go through repeat events to teach us, to humble us, to mold and fashion us, to develop our character and to make us who we are.

Life is a learning process and it is a series of choices. Sometimes we make good choices, and other time bad choices, but part of the purposes of these things, is to choose to do good or bad, to do the right thing or the wrong thing, and to ultimately turn **back** to our Creator, or **away** from Him. For this reason, things are repeatable, because God is long suffering and patient with us, to give us TIME to seek him and His own ways, rather than our own.

> "The Lord is not slack concerning his promise, as some men count slackness; but is ***longsuffering*** to us-ward, ***not willing that any should perish, but that all should come to repentance***." 2 Peter 3:9

God has given **time** for men to repent and follow him. Many people who do not believe in God, or simply choose not to follow Him, think life is just about **pleasure**. They selfishly pursue enjoyment and "Eat drink and be merry for tomorrow I die". What they fail to see is, they must give an account of their life after they die.

> "For we must all appear before the judgment seat of Christ, so that each of us may receive what is due us **for the things done while in the body, whether good or bad**." 2 Corinthians 5:10 (NIV)

Time vs Eternity

The binary flow of time and eternity is of great contrast! Time is temporary! Eternity is forever. Time is finite but eternity is infinite! Because the physical world is under the time restrains it is all temporary!

> "While we look not at the ***things which are seen***, but at the things which are not seen: for ***the things which are seen are temporal***; but the things which are not seen are ***eternal***." 1 Cor. 4:18

Not only does man have a time allotment, but everything physical, and everything visible, has a time allotment, and at some point, it will all come to an end. **The spiritual world (**things unseen**) are eternal** but **the visible world is temporary**. After the return of Christ, and after the millennial reign of Jesus on earth, the bible says God will create a new heaven and earth!

> "For behold, I will create ***new heavens*** and a ***new earth***. The former things will not be remembered, nor will they come to mind." Isaiah 65:17

Just as God used his **voice** to **speak the world into existence,** so will he **use his voice to shake the physical world, and remove it from existence:**

> "Whose ***voice*** then shook the earth: but now he hath promised, saying, Yet once more I shake not ***the earth*** only, but also ***heaven***. And this word, Yet once more, signifieth ***the removing of those things that are shaken***, as of ***things that are made***, that those things which cannot be shaken may remain." Hebrews 12:26-27

New Heaven and New Earth

God will speak, and it will cause the earth and its atmosphere, along with the starry universe (heavens), to be dissolved and burned by the heat of his fury! God will create a new earth and heaven that will not be subject to limitations, decay, or death, but will be as everlasting as the nature of God himself! **Time will end** and **eternity will begin!**

> "Looking for and hasting unto the coming of the day of God, wherein ***the heavens being on fire shall be dissolved***, and the ***elements shall melt with fervent heat***? Nevertheless we, according to his promise, look for ***new heavens and a new earth***, wherein dwelleth righteousness." 2 Peter 3:12-13

When this occurs, there will be no more division or disparity. When

Satan is thrown into the Lake of Fire, (which may be the universe which has been set afire by Gods voice), the demons and wicked men are joined with him. Only then, will there be peace and righteousness forever! Time will have been fulfilled. The sand will have run to the bottom of the hourglass and the timer will run out.

"He made known to us the mystery of his will according to his good pleasure, which he purposed in Christ, to be put into effect ***when the times reach their fulfillment***-to bring ***unity*** to all things in heaven and on earth under Christ." Ephesians 1:9-10

The Alpha and the Omega

"I am ***Alpha and Omega***, the ***beginning and the ending***, saith the Lord, which is, and which was, and which is to come, the Almighty." Revelation 1:8

"I am Alpha and Omega, the beginning and the end, **the first and the last**." Revelation 22:13

It is interesting that in both the **first** chapter of Revelation, and the **last** chapter of Revelation, both declare that Jesus is the **Alpha and the Omega**. This has often bothered me, because Jesus is eternal, whereas the alpha and omega mean the beginning and the end, or the First and the Last, meaning something finite. But the mystery of the Alpha and Omega is the very fact that Jesus entered the time frame of man and became a part of the fabric of our created world. He both created life, and yet became a part of his own creation. He, which was Spirit, became flesh, and the invisible became visible, and the spiritual became physical.

"That which was from ***the beginning***,(The Creator and the Alpha) which we have ***heard***, which we have ***seen*** with our eyes, which we have ***looked upon***, and our ***hands have handled***, of the Word of life; For the life was manifested, and we have seen it, and bear witness, and shew unto you that eternal life, which was with the Father, and was manifested unto us; That which we have seen and heard declare we unto you..." 1 John 1:1-3

"And the Word was ***made flesh***, and ***dwelt among us***, (and we beheld his glory, the glory as of the only begotten of the Father,) full of grace and truth." John 1:14

Jesus is the beginning and end because he **created time** and will **end time**. He created the heavens and earth and he will end their existence.

Jesus created the **first heavens and earth** and he will create the **last heavens and earth**. He will make all things new.

"And God shall wipe away all tears from their eyes; and there shall be no more death, neither sorrow, nor crying, neither shall there be any more pain: for the former things are passed away. And he that sat upon the throne said, Behold, ***I make all things new***. And he said unto me, Write: for these words are true and faithful. And he said unto me, It is done. I am Alpha and Omega, the beginning and the end." Revelation 21:4-6

The Great Timekeeper will close the old chapter of temporary man, and begin a new chapter on the eternal man, who will abide with him forever!

Chapter 17 - Punishment and Rewards – the Binary Code of Judgment

Consequences and Judgment!

Even from childhood we hopefully learn that our behavior has consequences. Sometimes as adults, I think we tend to either forget this, or think we have outgrown the silly notion of **consequences**.

As children we are answerable to our parents for our actions, but many do not understand that **as adults we are answerable to God!** If Satan can convince man that there is no God through atheism or evolution, then he can convince them that there is no moral standard but their own. In the sixties the slogan was "If it feels good, do it." Now the slogan today seems to be "You don't have a right to judge me." The thing is...God does!

> "For not from the east or from the west and not from the wilderness comes lifting up, ***but it is God who executes judgment***, putting down one and lifting up another" Psalms 75:6-7 (ESV)

We can never be answerable to man because he is flawed but must be answerable to God because he is perfect. God is our Creator and is righteous so ultimately, he is our judge. We can easily hide things from man, but **we can hide nothing from the eyes of God**!

> "For ***nothing is hidden***, except to be revealed; ***nor has anything been secret***, but that it would come to light." Mark 4:22 (NAS)

The debate over moral absolutes is not a philosophical one, nor is it answered in the lectures of the college class by amoral professors. It is answered solely in the book of the Bible. We have explained that man has been given a **moral compass** by God, and a **mosaic law** to remind us what is good and what is evil. He has also given us a **conscience** to guide us in the direction of that moral compass. Some simply refuse to follow it, and will harden their hearts, and some sadly will sear their conscience until they are void of one!

This however will not negate the **consequences** of our behavior but rather justify them! We will all have to answer for the deeds of our body whether good or bad.

Sowing and Reaping

There **will** be a judgment day when all sin will be judged, but **often we are judged in this life,** for many of the things we do. Some judgment will be reserved for judgment day at the end of our lives, but some come quickly in this life!

> "The sins of some men are quite evident, going before them to judgment; for others, their sins follow after." 1 Timothy 5:24 (NAS)

The judgment we receive in this life, can be either for correction or reward, and is through the binary principle of **sowing** and **reaping**.

> "Do not be deceived: God is not mocked, ***for whatever one sows, that will he also reap.*** For the one who sows ***to his own flesh*** will from the flesh reap corruption, but the one who sows ***to the Spirit*** will from the Spirit reap eternal life. And let us not grow weary of doing good, for in due season ***we will reap***, if we do not give up." Gal.6:7-9 (NIV)

The principle is that ***we will get back what we give out.*** Good seed produces good fruit, and bad seed produces bad fruit. Good actions will bring us a blessing, and evil actions a curse. It is sometimes called **the law of return**. Even the heathen have a word for it: **Karma**! If you treat others nicely, they will treat you well. If you treat them badly, don't expect others to treat you any differently!

Sowing is giving away. Not only does it matter what we give but how much. Even good things can be given selfishly and stinginess in giving to others will reap little!

> "Remember this: Whoever sows ***sparingly*** will also reap sparingly, and whoever sows ***generously*** will also reap generously" 2 Corinthians 9:6.

Jesus told the **parable of the sower,** who sowed seed into four different types of ground. The first was **The Wayside (or side of the path),** were men trod and where birds take up the seed before it can grow. Jesus said this is where the Devil takes away the word of God away before it can take root! Then there is **the Rocky ground,** where the soil is shallow and though the seed initially springs up, the rocky ground keeps the seed from growing. **The thorny ground** allows the plants to grow, but ultimately the thorns chokes the seed and kill it. Jesus said the thorns represent the **cares of this life** that choke up the word of God. Then finally there is the **Good ground** where not only does the seed grow up, but it multiplies thirty-fold, sixty-fold, and a hundred-fold!

So, the **binary system** is **good ground** and **bad ground**! This parable not only speaks of **two grounds**, but it refers to **four levels of growth.** The first level is **no growth**. The seed fell to the ground but immediately the Devil yanks it out of the heart and the person cannot believe. This represents no faith at all. It is a seed that produces nothing.

The second seed brings **little growth** because of the **rocky ground.** It springs up quickly and dies quickly because there are no roots. This is a Christian with **no foundation**. The rocky soil prevents the roots from growing. It looks good on the outside but is only top heavy because no roots anchor it to the ground and little water and nutrients get to the plant. It's like giving birth to a baby and then not feeding it. This is a baby Christian that does not grow. If one does not remove the old rocks of sin and personal stumbling blocks, he will not grow. Jesus said concerning the rocky ground, that he "**endures**" for a little while but when **tribulation or persecution** comes, he will fall away. These Christians only grow partially but are not strong enough to endure the difficulties of life!

The third level of growth brings the seed to full measure and maturity but then it starts to stagnate and then die! This Christian's faith grows beyond the infant stage and becomes spiritually mature, but the **Thorny ground** chokes their spiritual life and ultimately kills them. Jesus said these things are the **cares of life** and the **deceitfulness of riches**. Life is not about positions or possessions or comfort or concerns, but rather it is about the kingdom of God, not worldliness! These Christians may be full grown but ultimately produces no fruit and die!

The Good ground is the place that not only **grows up to its full statue** but **reproduces** themselves in others. It is fruitful in varying ways.

Jesus confirmed these four levels of growth in another parable:

> "And he said, So is the ***kingdom of God***, as if a man should cast ***seed*** into the ground; And should sleep, and rise night and day, and the seed should spring and grow up, he knoweth not how. For the earth bringeth forth fruit of herself; ***first the blade***, then ***the ear***, after that the ***full corn*** in the ear. But when the fruit is brought forth, immediately he putteth in the sickle, because the harvest is come." Mark 4:26-29

Here we see the **seed**, the **blade** (the first sprouting), the **ear** (the beginning of the produce and the full ear. The final **full corn**!

How does the binary code work in all this? Remember the binary code breaks down into its simplest state and looks for conflicting or opposing differences.

Though there are **four levels of growth** there ultimately are **only two. Growth or no growth. Fruitfulness or no fruitfulness**. This is Jesus point. We will either be fruitful or not.

> "Either make the ***tree good*** and its ***fruit good***, or else make ***the tree bad*** and its ***fruit bad***; for a tree is known by its fruit." Matthew 12:33

So, the binary code of fruit is either **good fruit or bad frui**t, a **good tree or a bad tree, fruitfulness or not fruitfulness**. We come full circle back again to the garden!

The same principle applies to **the ground**. The sower is the same: God. The seed is the same (God's word) but the only thing that is different is the ground. Although there are f**our types of ground**: wayside, rocky, thorny, and good, the binary system is that there **really is only two grounds: good ground or bad ground!** There are only **two types of hearts, receptive** and **non-receptive.** All mankind will either receive or reject the seed of God's truth!

Judgment of Words

The bible says we will give an account even for the words we say:

> "O generation of vipers, how can ye, being evil, speak good things? for out of the abundance of the heart the mouth speaketh. A good man out of the good treasure of the heart bringeth forth **good things**: and an evil man out of the evil treasure bringeth forth **evil things**. But I say unto you, That *every idle word that men shall speak, they shall give account thereof in the day of judgment*. For by thy words thou shalt be justified, and by thy words thou shalt be condemned." Matthew 12:34-37

What we speak determines our heart, and reveals its nature, either good or bad. For the words of our mouth speak the contents of our heart. Every idle word is recorded by God, and on Judgment Day our words will either **condemn us** or **acquit us**! Those who have spoken the Lords name in vain, or have allowed profanity to defile their heart, will give an account of those words. Those who gossip or speak ill of others, who mock or bully, or lie and bear false witness, will have their own word testify against them. Likewise, those who have praised God and blessed man, will be justified before God!

Conviction of Sin, Righteousness & Judgment

Jesus has sent the Holy Spirit to **convict** us of our **sins,** in order to bring us to repentance, It is not through condemnation, but to lovingly make us aware of what we have done, so that we might turn away from those things, that are displeasing in his sight. When we do, we will be **convinced** and assured of our **righteousness** by the Holy Spirit. If we do not repent, and turn from our sins, then the Holy Spirit will **convict** us of **judgment**, that is he will point out our guilt in our heart, and if we do not respond, he will warn us of judgment for those sins.

> "Nevertheless, I tell you the truth: it is to your advantage that I go away, for if I do not go away, the ***Helper*** will not come to you. But if I go, I will send him to you. And when he comes, ***he will convict the world concerning sin and righteousness and judgment***:" John 16:7-8

Jesus is our Judge

Allah will not judge man, nor Buddha, Krishna, or any other false God! Jesus alone, being God's Son, has been given the right to judge man, because he is their deliverer, and is righteous in judgment!

> "The Father judges no one, but has ***given all judgment to the Son***, that all may honor the Son, just as they honor the Father. Whoever does not honor the Son does not honor the Father who sent him. Truly, truly, I say to you, ***whoever hears my word and believes him who sent me has eternal life. He does not come into judgment but*** has passed from death to life. "Truly, truly, I say to you, an hour is coming, and is now here, when the dead will hear the voice of the Son of God, and those who hear will live. For as ***the Father*** has life in himself, so he has granted the Son also to have life in himself. And he ***has given him authority to execute judgment, because he is the Son of Man.*** Do not marvel at this, for an hour is coming when all who are in the tombs will hear his voice and come out, ***those who have done good to the resurrection of life, and those who have done evil to the resurrection of judgment.*** "I can do nothing on my own. As I hear, I judge, and ***my judgment is just,*** be-

> cause I seek not my own will but the will of him who sent me." John 5:22-30 (ESV)

Here we see two resurrections: The **Resurrection of Life** for the redeemed and the **Resurrection of judgment** for the wicked!

Binary Teachings of Jesus

Just as the **conduct** our lives will result in **blessing or curses,** the **culmination** of our life will result in **reward or punishment.** The judgment of God entails judging both the wicked and the righteous! The binary code is the system of **division** and **separation,** and in a series of **judgment** **parables,** Jesus gave analogies to show the **division** of the **wicked and the righteous!**

The Sheep and the Goats

Jesus said at his second coming He would gather the nations and would divide them into **two groups**. He said it was like a Shepherd that divides the **sheep from the goats,**

> "When the Son of man shall come in his glory, and all the holy angels with him, then shall he sit upon the throne of his glory: And ***before him shall be gathered all nations***: and ***he shall separate them one from another,*** as a shepherd divideth his ***sheep*** from the ***goats***: And he shall set the ***sheep on his right hand***, but ***the goats on the left.*** Then shall the King say unto them ***on his right hand, Come***, ye blessed of my Father, ***inherit the kingdom*** prepared for you from the foundation of the world." Matthew 25:31-34

Jesus is the good Shepherd, and he knows those who are His. Sometimes goats and sheep look similar, and even bleat the same way, but are quite different. A true shepherd knows what to look for! Goats have double coats of hair or mohair, and sheep have fleece or wool. Sheep tails lay downward, but goats tail stick upward. Goats have beards, and sheep have manes. Most goats have horns (unless bred to be without horns), sheep usually do not! Goats are independent, wild, and often curious, so are prone to wander, whereas sheep are mostly domesticated, and prefer to stay with the flock. Sheep feed on clover and grass, but goats eat twigs, vines shrubs, and just about anything! Goats and sheep are not even of the same species, and they have different chromosomes from each other! The parable is showing, that in the end time God will **separate** the saved from the unsaved. Oh! One other interesting fact! Goats scream but lambs don't!

The Wheat and the Tares!

Jesus also told a parable about **wheat** and **tares**! Tares are a **counterfeit wheat.** It is a **weedy** darnel, or rye grass, that **contain a noxious poison in it,** and is **bitter** in taste? They look remarkably similar to wheat, and the only way to tell the difference, is when it is full grown.

> "Another parable put he forth unto them, saying, The kingdom of heaven is likened unto a man which sowed ***good seed*** in his field: But while men slept, ***his enemy*** came and ***sowed tares among the wheat,*** and went his way. But when the blade was sprung up, and brought forth fruit, then appeared the tares also. So, the servants of the householder came and said unto him, Sir, didst not thou sow good seed in thy field? from whence then hath it tares? He said unto them, ***An enemy hath done this***. The servants said unto him, Wilt thou then that we go and gather them up? But he said, Nay; lest while ye gather up the tares, ye root up also the wheat with them. ***Let both grow together*** until the harvest: and ***in the time of harvest*** I will say to the reapers, ***Gather ye together first the tares, and bind them in bundles to burn them: but gather the wheat into my barn.***" Matthew 13:24-30

The enemy naturally is Satan, and the **tares are the wicked,** and the **wheat are the righteous**! In the harvest or end times, the angels will gather the righteous unto himself, but the wicked, like the tares, will be thrown into the fire (lake of fire!). This parable was explained to his disciples by Jesus himself, so there is no doubt about its meaning (Matthew 13:34-43)!

The Good and Bad Fish Caught in the Net!

Jesus always told parables to communicate to the people in a way they could relate to. Having several fishermen as disciples he told them this parable of the **net full of fish**.

> "Once again, the kingdom of heaven is like ***a net*** that was let down into the lake and caught ***all kinds of fish***. When it was full, the fishermen pulled it up on the shore. Then they sat down and ***collected the good fish in baskets*** but ***threw the bad away***. This is how it will be at the ***end of the age***. The angels will come and ***separate the wicked from the righteous*** and throw them into ***the fiery furnace,*** where there will be weeping and gnashing of teeth." Matthew 13:47-50 (NIV)

So again, we see this pattern of **gathering**, **separating the good** and **throwing away the bad.** The pattern of fiery judgment is clear. Those who choose to serve the devil willfully or not, will receive the same judgment as Satan and the fallen angels (demons)!

> "Then he will say to those on his left, 'Depart from me, you cursed, into the ***eternal fire prepared for the devil and his angels.***" Matthew 25:41 ESV

> "And the ***devil*** who had deceived them was thrown into ***the lake of fire and sulfur*** where the beast and the false prophet were, and they will be ***tormented day and night forever and ever***." Revelation 20:10 (ESV)

Other Contrasting Parables of Jesus!

The Wandering Sheep!

Though goats wander and run off a lot, occasionally sheep do too. Normally sheep like to stay with the herd for protection and many run from danger to the safety of the herd. Often shepherds use dogs to keep the herd together. This is because if one sheep starts to stray, the danger is that many will follow him. (Ever seen one or two people lead a whole section of a church astray or cause a division?) Elders must often act as sheepdogs and help keep the flock together!

Another problem with sheep is they tend to follow other sheep rather than the shepherd. Many shepherds have lost sheep because one will fall off a cliff and others will simply follow it! (they aren't always very bright!) We are to always follow Jesus and not just other Christians. Jesus told the parable of the Shepherd, leaving the ninety-nine to go rescue the one lamb that was lost, to illustrate his care for each individual. Whereas we would count the loss of one sheep as collateral damage, Jesus seeks to rescue the and return all those who are his! He left the multitude of angels in heaven, to go after the "lost sheep of Israel" (Matthew 15:24, Matthew 10:6)

The Prodigal and Privileged Sons

The parable of the Prodigal son (Luke 15:11-32) is really about **two sons**. They both had an inheritance but the younger one took his, left home, and lived in sin until he lost everything. He then had to humble himself and return to his father with the intent of being a servant instead of a son.

The point of the parable is God's willingness to forgive and willingly accept one when they return to Him! The other son stayed home and was faithful, but he became jealous and angry at his brother because his father gave him a robe a ring and a feast! The father told the older son that everything the father owned was available to him, but it was important to be joyful, that the younger brother had repented, and returned! But the message of this parable is about the **oldest son** as much as the **youngest son**! Jesus audience was to the Pharisees (**religious** leaders) as well as **sinners.** The message to the youngest son is grace and forgiveness, and the message to the oldest was not to trust in self-righteousness but to be grateful and receive whoever God accepts!

The Two Servants!

This parable is about **two servants,** though it is often called the parable of **the Unforgiving Servant** (Matthew 18:23-35)! The king required his servant to pay his debt of **ten thousand talents (50 million dollars),** and when he couldn't, the king was going to sell his wife and children into slavery, and sell all he had, to pay his debt. The servant fell on his knees and begged the king to be patient and he would pay him back. The king had mercy, and forgave his debt, and let him go. But then this servant came across one of his servants, who owed him **a hundred denarii (a few thousand dollars**) and demanded that he pay him. The man asked him to be patient, and he would pay him back, but the man said no, and threw him in jail. Jesus ends the parable with a clear explanation:

> "Then the master called the servant in. 'You wicked servant,' he said, '**I canceled all that debt of yours** because you begged me to. **Shouldn't you have had mercy on your fellow servant just as I had on you?**' In anger his master handed him over to the jailers to be tortured, until he should pay back all he owed." This is how my heavenly Father will treat each of you unless you forgive your brother or sister from your heart." Matthew 18:32-35 (NIV)

The King's servant was forgiven of a huge debt yet could not forgive someone that owed him a small debt.

Parable of the Laborers

In this parable (Matthew 20:1-16) a landowner hires laborer early in the morning to work in his vineyard for a denarius a day. Later that morning he hires some more workers and at noon. He hires some at 3 pm. He hires some at 5pm. At the end of the day, he gave them all a denarius. Naturally, the workers that worked all day were upset that the laborers who only worked only one hour got the same wages. The owner said that they got paid what they were promised, and that they should not be envious because he was being generous. This is a parable about **God's justice** vs **man's justice**! In the natural, it does seem like the ones who worked more should get more. But in **God's justice** he gives everybody the same not based upon the amount they work but on his own generosity. Again, it is about grace, because he gives what is owe to **the faithful,** but gives equally to **those who do not deserve it.** Man's sense of equality and fairness is different than God's. The last workers got a denarius for an hour's work, so the other workers thought that they were going to get a denarius an hour, but the owner only promised a denarius a day. They were overtaken by **greed** rather than **gratefulness**. Those workers who worked all day were unemployed, and the owner came by and offered them a job. At the end of the day they were unthankful and angry because they worked longer and harder which is true, but they got what was promised.

Jesus ended with saying "***the first will be last and the last will be first!***" Have you ever been the last picked in sports or the last chosen for a task? It could very well be that those chosen last were the least capable of working. The owner may have just been gracious to help them out. This is certainly consistent with the nature of God! Jesus sought out the tax collectors, prostitutes, the sick, and lame, and reached out to the dregs of society at the anger of the religious leaders. This parable can also be about the two binary groups; the **downcast** and the **privileged**!

The Two Sons

"What do you think? There was a man who had ***two sons***. He went to the first and said, 'Son, **go and work** today in the vineyard.' '**I will not**,' he answered, but later he **changed his mind and went**. "Then the father went to the other son and said the same thing. He answered, '**I will**, sir,' **but he did not go**."Which of the two did what his father wanted?" "The first," they answered. Jesus said to them, "Truly I tell you, the tax collectors and the prostitutes are entering the kingdom of God ahead of you. For John came to you to show you the way of righteousness, and you did not believe him, but the tax collectors and the prostitutes did. And even after you saw this, you did not repent and believe him." Matthew 21:28-32 (NIV)

This is a similar binary parable that teaches **contrasting attitudes** of **two sons**. Jesus was saying that *one son represented the* ***religious leaders***, and the *other son represented the* ***repentant sinner***. Jesus teaches that the least esteemed of society that obey God are greater than those who give him lip service. He said of them.

> "'You hypocrites! Isaiah was right when he prophesied about you: These ***people honor me with their lips, but their hearts are far from me.***" Matthew 15:8 (NIV)

The Faithful vs. The Wicked Servant

Matthew 24:45-51

Another contrasting parable is that of **two servants** of a master, One, was faithful to take care of the master's household while he had to go away! The Wicked servant however thinks that since the Master has been gone for a long time, he may not return so he beats the other servants and becomes a drunkard. He does not take care of the master's household or possessions so when the Master returns at a time that he wasn't expected, he kills him and sends him to a place of weeping and gnashing of teeth – **hell**! (Matthew13:42). This parable speaks of the Pharisees and Sadducees who were to be the caretakers of God's people but were wicked servants and hypocrites. It speaks of his first coming, but I believe it also is speaking of his second coming. We know that just before his second coming there will be a great falling away and already, we are seeing compromises made by many pastors and religious leaders.

Jesus gave many other binary parables that showed contrasting lessons.

The Two Births and the Two Deaths

Another binary mystery is that there are **two births** and **two deaths**. We are all physically born naturally through the womb and come forth with a physical body, but Jesus said you must be born again. This greatly confused Nicodemus, a Jewish rabbi, because he did not understand, that one birth is physical, and one is spiritual.

"There was a man of the Pharisees, named ***Nicodemus***, a ruler of the Jews: The same came to Jesus by night, and said unto him, Rabbi, we know that thou art a teacher come from God: for no man can do these miracles that thou doest, except God be with him. Jesus answered and said unto him, Verily, verily, I say unto thee, ***Except a man be born again, he cannot see the kingdom of God.*** Nicodemus saith unto him, How can a man be born when he is old? can he enter the second time into his ***mother's womb***, and be born? Jesus answered, Verily, verily, I say unto thee, ***Except a man be born of water and of the Spirit,*** he cannot enter into the kingdom of God. That which is born of the flesh is ***flesh***; and that which is born of the Spirit is ***spirit***. Marvel not that I said unto thee, Ye must be born again. The wind bloweth where it listeth, and thou hearest the sound thereof, but canst not tell whence it cometh, and whither it goeth: so is every one that is born of the Spirit. Nicodemus answered and said unto him, How can these things be? Jesus answered and said unto him, Art thou a master of Israel, and knowest not these things?" John 3:1-10

Jesus said we must be born of **water** and **Spirit**. We are carried in our womb for nine months in what is called an **amniotic sac,** which is filled with **amniotic fluid**. This is commonly called water because it is mostly water with a small percent of protein and other nutrients. Matter of fact, the root word "***amni***" in amniotic is Latin meaning "**water**". This fluid surrounds, cushions, protects, and feeds the baby! When one is ready to give birth this sack breaks which starts the inducing of labor or contractions. The breaking of the amniotic sac is commonly called "**the water breaking**". So, we are **born of water**.

Jesus said that which is born of flesh is **flesh** but that which is born of Spirit is spirit. The **new or second birth** is a **spiritual birth.** It is where the human spirit is **born into the kingdom of God.** This is why Jesus said you must be born again, to see the kingdom of God! (John 3:3)

Just as there are two births, so there are also **two deaths!**
We are all **appointed** to physically die. Since Adam sinned, death came to all mankind because all men sin. **Physical death** is the **separation of the soul from the body**, and **spiritual death** is the **separation of the soul from God.**

"But the cowardly, unbelieving, abominable, murderers, sexually immoral, sorcerers, idolaters, and all liars shall have their part in the lake which burns with fire and brimstone, which is ***the second death.***" Revelation 21:8 (NKJV)

Jesus warned the early church, that many would be martyred, but he said this concerning both deaths:

"Fear none of those things which thou shalt suffer: behold, the devil shall cast some of you into prison, that ye may be tried; and ye shall have tribulation ten days: be thou faithful ***unto death***, and I will give thee a crown of life. He that hath an ear, let him hear what the Spirit saith unto the churches; He that overcometh shall not be hurt of the ***second death.*** " Revelation 2:10

Here we see both deaths, but he encouraged them that though some may physically **die once,** they would not be hurt by the **second death!**

The second death is the final judgment. It is the casting away eternally of the damned along with the Devil and fallen angels (demons).

"And the sea gave up the dead which were in it; and ***death and hell*** delivered up the dead which were in them: and they were ***judged*** every man according to their works. And ***death and hell were cast into the lake of fire. This is the second death.*** " Revelation 20:13-14

The judgment of Sodom and Gomorrah is a type of the Judgment of God. Just as God took Lot and his family out of the city before he destroyed it, so will he take his righteous out of the earth through the rapture, before he destroys it. The bible says the fire raining upon the city is a type of the judgment by fire upon the earth.

"Just as ***Sodom and Gomorrah*** and the surrounding cities, which likewise ***indulged in sexual immorality and pursued unnatural desire,*** serve as an ***example*** by undergoing a punishment of ***eternal fire***." Jude 1:7 (ESV)

The Reward of the Righteous!

"And, behold, I come quickly; and ***my reward is with me***, to give every man according as his work shall be." Revelation 22:12

While the **punishment** for sin is **eternal separation from God** and **spiritual death** in the lake of fire, the reward for the believers is the opposite, to abide with Jesus forever and **eternal life.**

"They will suffer the punishment of eternal destruction, ***away from the presence of the Lord*** and from the glory of his might." 2 Thessalonians 1:9 (ESV)

The final judgment whether **punishment or reward** is eternal

"And these shall go away into ***everlasting punishment***: but the righteous into ***life eternal***." Matthew 25:46

The Two Resurrections

The bible speaks of two resurrections: "**The Resurrection of Life**" and "**the Resurrection of Judgment**." These two resurrections are referred to as the resurrection of those who have done **good** and those who have done **evil** (like the Tree in the Garden!).

> "Do not be amazed at this, for the hour is coming when all who are in their graves will hear His voice and come out—those who have done ***good*** to the ***resurrection of life***, and those who have done ***evil*** to the ***resurrection of judgment***." John 5:28 (NIV)

> "And have hope toward God, which they themselves also allow, that there shall be a ***resurrection of the dead***, both of the ***just*** and ***unjust***." Acts.24:15

Jesus was the first to rise from the grave and conquer death. His resurrection is called the **first fruit,** but afterwards, he will raise the righteous from the dead. **Some will be raised in the Rapture, and others at his second coming.** But this resurrection is the **resurrection of life and** will be rewarded with **eternal life**.

> "But ***Christ*** has indeed been ***raised from the dead***, the ***firstfruits*** of those who have fallen asleep. For ***since death came through a man, the resurrection of the dead comes also through a man***. For as in Adam all die, so in Christ all will be made alive. But each in his own turn: ***Christ the firstfruits; then at His coming, those who belong to Him***" 1 Co.15:20-23 (NIV)

Before the thousand-year reign of Christ on earth, God will also raise up the martyrs, who died during the seven-year rule of the Antichrist. They will co-reign on the earth with Christ. This also is part of the **first resurrection.**

> "And I saw thrones, and they sat upon them, and judgment was given unto them: and I saw the souls of them that were ***beheaded for the witness of Jesus***, and for the word of God, and which had not worshiped the beast, neither his image, neither had received his mark upon their foreheads, or in their hands; and they lived and reigned with Christ a thousand years. But the rest of the dead lived not again until the thousand years were finished. This is the ***first resurrection***. Blessed and holy is he that hath part in the ***first resurrection***: on such the ***second death*** hath no power, but they shall be priests of

God and of Christ and shall reign with him a thousand years." Revelation 20:4 -6

The **righteous** will resurrect **first** before the Millennial reign of the Lord! The **wicked** will then be resurrected **after** the millennial reign of Christ and then they will be judged and punished for their wickedness. This is the **Second resurrection**!

The Two Books

The binary system of judgment continues with the mystery of **the Two Books!** There are **two books** mentioned in the bible. In the Great White throne Judgment, the wicked are judged by a **Book of Remembrance** (perhaps a set of books), which is perhaps the lists of deeds of the wicked. The other book is the **Book of Life** and their destiny is based simply on **if their name is in it!**

"And I saw a great white throne, and him that sat on it, from whose face the earth and the heaven fled away; and there was found no place for them. And I saw the dead, small and great, stand before God; and ***the books were opened***: and another book was opened, which is ***the book of life***: and the dead were judged out of those things which were written in ***the books***, according to their works. And the sea gave up the dead which were in it; and death and hell delivered up the dead which were in them: and they were judged every man ***according to their works.***" Revelation 20:11:12

The prophet Malachi spoke of this Book (or set of book collectively) called the **Book of Remembrance!**

"Then those who feared the Lord spoke with one another. The Lord paid attention and heard them, and ***a book of remembrance was written*** before him of those who feared the Lord and esteemed his name." They shall be mine, says the Lord of hosts, in the day when I make up my treasured possession, and I will spare them as a man spares his son who serves him. Then once more you shall see ***the distinction between the righteous and the wicked, between one who serves God and one who does not serve him.***" Malachi 3:16-18 (ESV)

This chapter in Malachi is about the second coming of Messiah. It refers to the Lord coming for judgment! It asks earlier in the Chapter **"*Who***

can endure the day of his coming? Who can stand when he appears?" The Messiah declares in this chapter that he will come near for judgment. This **Book of Remembrance** is set before him and through it he will judge mankind. All our actions and words that will either accuse us or excuse us have been written down. Those deeds and words will either condemn us or justify us!

> "For God shall bring ***every work into judgment***, with every secret thing, ***whether it be good, or whether it be evil***." Ecclesiastes 12:14

Even the old testament has many references to **God's judgment Books:** *(Ex. 32:32,* Psalm *56:8 Dan. 7:9-10, Dan.12:1*)

The other book is **The Book of Life.** Everyone who is a believer has his name written in this book, and the ones who are not saved are not written in this book, which will also determine the final judgment and destiny of the wicked.

> "And all that dwell upon the earth shall worship him, whose names are not written in ***the book of life*** of the Lamb slain from the foundation of the world." Revelation 13:8

> "And death and hell were cast into the lake of fire. This is the second death. And whosoever was not found written in ***the book of life*** was cast into the lake of fire." Revelation 20:14-15

When the disciples cast out demons in Jesus name, they were astonished at the power they had, but Jesus said that their **position** was far greater than their **power**!

> "Nevertheless, do not rejoice in this, that the spirits are subject to you, but rejoice that ***your names are recorded in heaven.***" Luke 10:20 (NAS)

This recording of names is the list of the redeemed in the **Book of Life!**
I do not want to argue for or against eternal security but simply want to point out that it does often mention **being put into the book of life and yet being able to be blotted out as well as not being written in the book of Life!** I will leave that to the reader to make their own conclusion.

> "Add iniquity unto their iniquity: and let them not come into thy righteousness. ***Let them be blotted out of the book of the living***, and not be written with the righteous. Psalm69:27-28

> "He that overcometh, the same shall be clothed in white raiment; and ***I will not blot out his name out of the book of life***, but I will confess his name be-

fore my Father, and before his angels. He that hath an ear, let him hear what the Spirit saith unto the ***churches***." Revelation 3:5,6

Every man must appear before God to give an account of their lives.

"For we must all appear before the judgment seat of Christ, so that each one may receive what is due for what he has done in the body, ***whether good or evil***. 2 Corinthians 5:10

The binary code is a cyclical code. It often comes full circle in symbolism. We started out in the Garden with the two trees, the **Tree of the Knowledge of good and evil** and the **Tree of Life,** and we end up with the final judgment of a **book of deeds good or evil** and a **book of Life!** So, the essence of the two trees was not just Adam and Eve's choice, but it is symbolic of **every man's choice!** Choose the tree that leads to sin, or the Tree that leads to **eternal life!**

Chapter 18 - Summary and Conclusion

As we have seen throughout this book, the Binary Code of God is a series of binary systems that sometimes **oppose** each other and sometimes **compliment** each other. We see this code revealed in the **creation** of man to the **fall of man**; the **sin nature of man** to the **redemption of man**; the **blessing of mankind** and the **curses of mankind**; the **hope of men** and the **judgment of men; the origin of Satan and sin** to the **finality of the righteous and the wicked.** This code has been in operation to point man to the right choices and the right destination. Too many, it seems, think that God is far off and far removed from us, but not only is He directly involved in our life, but he is the architect of our life, and therefore has left us with a blueprint to guide us throughout our lives.

God is all about cyclical patterns, that often repeat. They are here to show us the duality of life, and the contrasts of human events, that convey two distinctions of good and evil, God's ways or the Devils, God's purposes or our own! We learn from these examples that the binary principles are revealing a mystery and conveying a meaning. The bible has been given to us by God himself to understand the existing **polar opposites** of things like **light and darkness, good and evil, right and wrong, law and grace, and heaven or hell.**

The Two Foundations

Many of Jesus parables also give us examples of principles of division and separation, such as: two paths, goats and sheep, good fish and bad fish; good ground and bad ground, good fruit and bad fruit, etc. In another binary contrast Jesus gave an interesting parable of **two foundations:**

> "Therefore whosoever ***heareth these sayings*** of mine, and ***doeth*** them, I will liken him unto a ***wise man***, which built his house upon a <u>***rock***</u>: And the ***rain*** descended, and the ***floods*** came, and the ***winds blew, and beat upon that house; and it fell not:*** for it was founded upon a rock. And every one that ***heareth*** these sayings of mine, and ***doeth them not***, shall be likened unto a

foolish man, which built his house upon the __*sand*__: And the ***rain*** descended, and the ***floods*** came, and the ***winds blew, and beat upon that house; and it fell:*** and great was the fall of it." Matthew 7:24-27

This amazing binary parable tells us of **two people, two actions, two decisions and two different results**. Jesus tells of **two builders** who built houses, one on **rock**, and one on **sand**! It doesn't matter whose house was bigger or better or more expensive. It matters not about how good they looked or how long they took to build it, or whether they were Mansions or shacks.But it did matter **how long they stood,** What really mattered is not the building but **the foundation**, One was **wisely built on a rock foundation** and one was **foolishly built on slippery sand**! It is sort of like the kid's story of the three little pigs. Wood and straw fell to the wolve's wind, but the brick house stood! In this parable they both encountered the rain, the flood, and the winds. The house that was anchored to the rock stood but the one built on the sand fell!

You may ask yourself who would build their house on sand. In the city of Caesarea, Herod the Great build a great artificial harbor off the coastline. The Romans had invented a new kind of cement, that was mixed with volcanic ash, and it could harden underwater. Herod used this technology to construct giant piers, warehouses and towers jetting out into the sea by building giant boxes and filling them with this concrete. The city took 10 years to build and became a marvelous ancient seaport. However, the whole concrete harbor was built on sand instead of bedrock, and it was later destroyed by underwater quakes. Virtually nothing is left today of the great harbor.

Jesus is likening these two foundations to two kinds of people, those who **hear and obey** his words, and those who **hear and ignore** his words. So will it be for all mankind. Jesus words hold true. We must be wise in what we listen to and whom we obey.

The New Binary System

So, we must patiently pursue God, and wait for that glorious day, when he will create **a new binary system**; a **new heaven and a new earth,** where tears will be no more and heartache not even a memory. The **temporary** will turned into the **eternal!** The **tainted and defiled** will become **pure and holy! Hate** will be banished, and God's **love** will fill his people. The **Joy of the Lord** will replace all **worldly sorrow,** and **pleasure** will replace all **pain**! **Intimacy** with our Redeemer will replace **separation,** and eternal

fellowship will replace **isolation and loneliness**.

The **ban from the garden of Eden** shall be eternally lifted, and **heavens gates will be opened** to all who have come back to their God! Where in times past, we fought with **devils,** we now will walk with **angels**. **Dusty roads** will give way to **golden streets,** and the scourge of **death** will give way to **the Tree and the River of life**. There shall be no more **curse,** only the **blessing of eternal happiness** and no more **darkness,** only the **light of the presence of God!**

The timekeeper may blow the trumpet any moment and the return of Jesus will begin to usher the demise of all things wicked and evil. In the last few words of the bible there is a binary warning to man:

> "And he saith unto me, Seal not the sayings of the prophecy of this book: for the time is at hand. He that is ***unjust***, let him be unjust still: and he which is ***filthy***, let him be filthy still: and he that is ***righteous***, let him be righteous still: and he that is ***holy***, let him be holy still. And, behold, I come quickly; and my reward is with me, to give every man according as his work shall be. I am Alpha and Omega, the beginning and the end, the first and the last." Revelation 22:10-13

Rightly Dividing the Word

> "Study to shew thyself approved unto God, a workman that needeth not to be ashamed, rightly **dividing** the word of truth." 1 Timothy 2:15

This book has been about **the division of two things** and the understanding of our choice between **truth or error, righteousness or sin, obedience or disobedience, ourselves, or our Savior.** We all must choose the path we take, either the wide road that leads to destruction, or the narrow path that leads to eternal life. **The Binary Code** is simple but the execution of it can be difficult. Life is not merely about pleasure and personal pursuits. That was the choice of Adam and Eve when they tasted the delicious fruit of the tree of knowledge of good and evil. But life is really about recognizing our hereditary sin from that tree and repenting, so we can finally eat from the Tree of Life in the kingdom of God. (Rev.2:7).

There were **two** plans. Even as the Devil had his plan to destroy mankind, God had prepared a way of escape long before the foundations of the world. He knew how man would choose, so God set in motion His plan of Redemption:

> "But when the ***set time*** had fully come, ***God sent his Son***, born of a woman, born under the law, to redeem those under the law, that we might receive adoption to sonship. Because you are his sons, God sent the Spirit of his Son

into our hearts, the Spirit who calls out, "Abba, Father." So, you are no longer a slave, but God's child; and since you are his child, God has made you also an heir." Galatians 4:4 (NIV)

God sent **his Son,** so that we would become **his sons by adoption**, and not merely his creation. He would adopt any who would turn to him, and be a heavenly Father not just a Creator; not just a distant deity, but a personal God and an intimate God. His motivation was not power, prestige or mere worship, because he had all these before with the angels. His motivation was love for mankind, his favorite creation. God so Loved the world he gave.... Jesus. Jesus sacrifice was the only thing sufficient enough to warrant the removal of sin, and bring us back into the heavenly garden, the Paradise of his presence and the fellowship of eternity!

Life is about **two choices, decisions and destinations**! **Accept** or **ignore**! **Believe** or **doubt**. **Follow** or **be left behind**. **Obey** or **disobey**! **Receive** or **reject**! **Turn** or **burn**! Choose **eternal life** or **eternal punishment**; **eternal rest** or **everlasting torment**; choose to go **up** or you will be going **down**; choose **heaven** or the choice will be **hell**! End up with **Jesus** or end up with **Satan**! God has clearly shown us the **truth,** yet some prefer the **lie**.

Accept Jesus as Lord and he will prepare a place for you and come again and receive you unto himself. Gods binary code is simple to see, and it's intent is to show us the only way unto himself.

Jesus had **two comings** with **two purposes,** but time is short, and every person will in the end, resurrect to only **one outcome**. As we await his coming, he awaits your choice!

Maranatha!

Binary Charts

Chapter 1 -Chart 1

Chapter One-The Two Armies-The Binary Code in Heaven		
The First Day of Creation		***Notes***
Heavens (atmosphere, Starry Space, Heavenly Realm of God)	**Earth** (undeveloped planet)	**First Binary System Of Creation:** Heavenly system - Earthly system
Light Day Morning	**Darkness** Night Evening	Created Light Divided Light from Darkness
Time Space Matter	In the Beginning The Heavens The Earth	**The Creation of Physical Realm** Basic Environment for Mankind
The Second Day of Creation		***Notes***
Firmament (Watery Dome) Heaven Waters Above	**Water** Waters on the earth Waters Below	Atmospheric Sky - Earthly Waters Divides Waters from Waters Oxygen and Water (essential for life)
Fountains of the Sky	**Fountains of the Deep** (earth)	Genesis 7:11
	Mist from the earth watered the whole face of the ground	(Water Vapor Or Water Evaporation Cycle.) Genesis 2:5-6
The Third Day of Creation		***Notes***
Earth Dry land	**Seas** Waters under the heavens (sky)	Division of land and Oceans
Seed, Grass, Fruit Trees		Food and Oxygen for Man
The Fourth Day of Creation		***Notes***
Lights in the firmament of the heavens Planets, Stars and Heavenly Bodies		To Give Light on the Earth For Signs, Seasons, Days and Years (TIME)
Sun (The Greater Light)	**Moon** (The Lesser Light)	**Two Great Lights**
Day	Night	To divide Day from Night
The Fifth Day of Creation		***Notes***
Sky and over the Earth	**Oceans**	Two divers habitations for Sky & Sea animals Wings and Gills
Winged Birds & Flying Creatures	Sea Creatures	
The Sixth Day of Creation		***Notes***
Land Inhabitants		
Land Animals	**Man**	To multiply and populate the earth
Cattle and creeping thing and beast of the earth	In God's image	Each according to their Kind (species)
Food and Sacrifices	Has Dominion over all creatures	Animals first and Man last!
Male and Female	Male and Female	Binary genders
Man named the animals	God named Adam	(Adam named Eve)
Binary Companions		"**Not good** for Man to be alone"
Adam	Eve	Mankind
Created for God	Created for Adam	Shared Dominion

Chapter 1 -Chart 2

Chapter One-The Two Armies-The Binary Code in Heaven		
Made from dust and Breath of God	Made from Adam's body (rib)	Different Chromasones "Woman" means "taken out of Man"
A Part from Him	A part of Him	
Two arms and two legs, two eyes, two ears, two hands, two feet, two nostrils, two breasts. Woman have two ovaries and men two testicles lungs, kidneys, and adrenal glands. Man also has two sets of ribs!		**Binary parts**
The Seventh Day of Creation		
Rest	Work	Two contrasting principles of Labor
Finished work	Adam worked in the Garden	Sabbath is completion of cycle
Enjoy results of work	Purpose in labor	Pleasure and satisfaction
Recreation	Creation	God's Sabbath an example for man
Reflection	accomplishment	"It is Good"
The Binary Trees in the Garden		**Binary Decisions**
Tree of Life	**Tree of the Knowledge of Good and Evil**	Good Fruit and Bad Fruit
Permitted access	Forbidden	Obedience and disobedience Free will and Two choices
Eternal Life	Death (Spiritual & Physical)	Consequence
Spiritual Death	**Physical Death**	
The spirit of man from God	The soul of Man from the body	Separation
Temptation in the Garden		
Serpent	**Eve**	Separated from Adam
Subtle more than any other creature	Naive	
Questions God's Word "Hath God said"	**Eve adds to Gods Word** "You shall not touch it	
Lies to Eve "You shall not die" "You shall be as Gods"	Believes the lies Begins to doubt Not content to know God	Division from the Truth Doubt vs Faith Pride comes before a fall
Introduces evil	Enticed by the fruit	Already had knowledge of good
Sin and its Consequences		**Fall of Adam and Eve**
Action	**Results**	
Ate of the Fruit	Eyes were opened	Saw they were naked and exposed
Saw that they were naked and exposed!	Made clothes out of fig leaves to cover their nakedness	Human effort to covering their sins. God slew animals and covered them with skins so **blood** could atone
Hid from God "Adam where are you?"	Fear of Punishment "I was afraid"	God chastises and pronounces curses
Eve listened to the Devil	Curse is Pain in labor in birth	
Adams listened to his wife	Ground is Cursed. Now work is hard an produce unyielding!	Enmity now between Satan and Man

Chapter 2 -Chart 1

Chapter One-The Two Armies-The Binary Code in Heaven		
The Fall of Lucifer (Then and Now)		***Ezekiel 28 and Isaiah 14***
Anointed Cherub (Angel)	Created being (Not son of God)	***Ezekiel 28***
Perfection "perfect in thy ways"	Corruption "iniquity was found in thee."	Ezekiel 28:15
Lucifer (Shining one, Morning Star, light bearer)	**Satan,** the Devil, the old Serpent. (the fallen one, The adversary, One who resists, Opposer!)	Change in Name Rev.12:7,1 Pet. 5;8
Beautiful ans adorned	Pride in himself	
Angel of Light	Prince of Darkness	
Sought to Praise God	Seeks personal Power	
You are	I will	
Unity with Angels	Division among the Angels	
At peace with God	At War with God	
Pure and holy	Defiled and impure	
Submissive and humble	Rebellious, Ambitious and proud	
Good and obedient	Evil and disobedient	Nature changed
Before God in Throneroom	Fallen to the earth	Change in Position
Once above	Now below	
Dominion in Heaven	Domain in Hell	
Jesus saw Lucifer fall from heaven to earth. (Like 10:18)	Satan saw Jesus resurrect and ascend to heaven	
God is truth	Father of lies, Liar from the beginning	
Believed	Deceived	
Personal Character The Seven I Am's of Jesus	Ambition/action The Five I wills of Lucifer	
Christ (Real Messiah	Antichrist (Counterfeit Messiah	Messiah and false messiah
Angelic War in heaven	Human and demonic War on earth	

Chapter 3 -Chart 1

Chapter 3 - The Two Choices – The Binary Code of Free Will		
The Angels-Only Two Choices		***notes***
Loyalty to God	Allegiance to Lucifer	
Obey God	Disobey God	
War with Satan	War with God	
Keep position in Heaven	Kicked out if heaven	Consequences
Adam and Eve-Only Two Choices		***notes***
Tree of Life	Tree of Knowledge of Good and Evil	Binary choice of Sin and righteousness
Obey God	Disobey	
Ignore Satan's lies	Listen to Satan	
Reject temptation	Give in to temptation	
Pure human race	Tainted human DNA	
innocence	Awareness of evil (Eyes were opened)	Consequence of Choice
No Guilt	Guilty conscience (Aware of nakedness Nakedness)	Hid from God
Faith in God Acceptance	Fear of God Punishment	Awareness of nakedness
Reward for Obedience	Punishment for disobediantce	
Covering of Animal Skins Gods garment by blood GRACE	Covering of Fig leaves Human self-made garments WORK	
Choice leads to nature of God or Satan		***notes***
Love (God is Love)	Hate (Satan's nature)	Hate stirs up Strife and division (Pro. 10:12) Love unites and unifies
Gives (John 3:16) unselfish	Takes (steals, covets) selfish in nature	Love looks to others Hate looks to self
Seeks after Peace	Causes war	
Love seeks the truth	Hate blinds men to the truth	
Love seeks life	Hate often leads to murder	
First children of Adam and Eve: Choice of first Binary Brothers: Genesis 4		***notes***
Abel (second child)	Cain (firstborn)	First will be last!
Shepherd Domesticated animals for food and offerings)	Farmer (cultvated cursed ground like his Father!)	

Chapter 3 -Chart 2

Chapter 3 - The Two Choices – The Binary Code of Free Will		
Offered animal sacrifice to God	Offered produce from cursed ground	
Blood Sacrifices As revealed by God clothing Adam and Eve in animal skins	Bloodless sacrifice Imitating parents covering by produce (fig leaves without blood!	Gods way vs Mans way
Life is in the blood	Death is in the ground	
Sacrifice accepted	Sacrifice rejected	
" If you do what is right, will you not be accepted?"	***"But if you do not do what is right, sin is crouching at your door "***	Clear right and wrong leads to acceptance or rejection (sin)! Genesis 4:7 NIV
Injustice (Dies at the hand of brother)	Cain **murdered** his brother Abel because of jealousy	(Cain acted on the nature of Satan who also was driven by jealousy of God)
	Cain **lied** to God about not knowing where Abel was	Satan is father of lies
Blood of Abel cried out to God (no cessation of life or consciousness after death	Able now cursed by the ground and would now yield little produce from the ground	Binary Double curse of the ground, First by Adam and second by Cain
"You must rule over it it!"	"Sin is crouching at the door"	Two choices concerning temptation and sin! Rule over it or let it in!
	Would now be a wanderer and vagabond upon the earth! (Land of **Nod** -means wandering)	As Satan was banished from heaven and Adam and Eve were banished from the Garden nor Cain banned from his family and the presence of the Lord!
	Marked by God as cursed by God	A warning and example to others!

Chapter 4 -Chart 1

Chapter 4 - The Two Paths_ The Binary Code of Direction		
The binary direction-THE TWO WAYS		***notes***
HORIZONTAL East and West Left or Right	VERTICAL North and South Up or Down	Physical and spiritual directions
Backwards	Foward	
RIGHT Right handed	LEFT Left handed	TWO SIDES Predominance
Jesus at the Right -Hand of God		
WISDOM "A **wise** man's heart inclines him to the **right**...."	FOOLISHNESS "...but a **fool's** heart to the **left**."	Ecclesiastes 10:2 (ESV)
SHEEP on the right Believers	GOATS on the left Unbelievers	Division of the nations Matt. 25:31-33
Repentant thief Went to Paradise with Christ	**Unrepentant thief** Went to hell without Christ	The TWO Thieves on the Cross
The binary destinations: THE TWO ROADS and PATHS		***Matthew 7:13-14***
TWO GATES	**TWO PATHS**	Entrances and direction
The **Wide** Gate	The **Broad** Road to Destruction	
The **Small** Gate	The **Narrow** Road to Life.	
Few travel on (minority go to heaven)	**Many** travel on (Majority go to hell)	Contrast of volume of people
Path to Heaven	Path to Hell	Contrast of direction of people
Path of Righteousness	Path of Sin	Contrast of morality of people
The Flood On Eight Survived	**Sodom and Gomorrah** Only 3 survived	**EXAMPLES** Minority rescued, Majority died **Many** are called but **few** are chosen!
The two Motions – FOWARD AND BACKWARDS		
FORWARD	BACKWARDS	
Towards something Walking towards God	Away from something Walking Away from God	Physical Spiritual
Depth (Committed to) Deep walk with God	Shallowness (Uncommitted) Superficial walk with God	3D axis (Height, width, **depth**)
"**Come unto me**" (Matt.11:28) "Draw near to God " (James 4:8)	**"Depart from me**!" (Matt. 7:23) Backslide-Fall away	Spiritual condition = Spiritual position Return or Depart
"**Come boldly** before my throne." Heb. 4:16	Adam **hid** from the presence of God (Gen. 3:10)	
Righteousness draws near with a clear conscience	Sin separates and pushes us away from God because of guilt	
ARRIVALS	DEPARTURES	EXAMPLE- airport

Chapter 4 -Chart 2

Chapter 4 - The Two Paths_ The Binary Code of Direction		
Will arrive in heaven after death, resurrection or Rapture	Will leave earth in death, resurrection or Rapture	
Will move **towards God** and **away from the world.**	Will move **towards the world** and **away from God**	
Time only moves **forward**		
The Binary Vertical directions – UP AND DOWN		***notes***
UP	**DOWN**	
Heaven	Hell	
ascend	descend	Jesus after his Death and Resurrection **(Eph. 4:10**
Rise upward	Fall downward	
Moses came **up**	**God came down**	Mount Sinai
Consecration	Desecration	
Smoke rises upward animal sacrifices worship Prayer		Examples rise upwards
Altar of Incense coals and smoke Prayers of the saints		Symbolism
Lift up Holy Hands Lift up your Voice		Praise and worship directed upward towards God! Hosea 8:1; Joel 2:1 2 Chronicles 5:13

Chapter 5 -Chart 1

Chapter 5 - The Two Consequences- the Binary Code of Blessing and Curses		
Blessings and Curses -*Deuteronomy 28*		
BLESSINGS 2 And **all these blessings** shall come on thee, and overtake thee, if thou shalt hearken unto the voice of the Lord thy God.	CURSES 15 But it shall come to pass, if thou wilt not hearken unto the voice of the Lord thy God, to observe to do all his commandments and his statutes which I command thee this day; that **all these curses** shall come upon thee, and overtake thee:	***Binary Consequences for obedience or disobedience to observing God's commandments***
3 Blessed shalt thou be in the city, and blessed shalt thou be in the field.	16 Cursed shalt thou be in the city, and cursed shalt thou be in the field.	Location
4 Blessed shall be the fruit of thy body, and the fruit of thy ground, and the fruit of thy cattle, the increase of thy kine, and the flocks of thy sheep.	18 Cursed shall be the fruit of thy body, and the fruit of thy land, the increase of thy kine, and the flocks of thy sheep.	Life and livelihood
5 Blessed shall be thy basket and thy store.	17 Cursed shall be thy basket and thy store.	Food and Possessions
6 Blessed shalt thou be when thou comest in, and blessed shalt thou be when thou goest out.	19 Cursed shalt thou be when thou comest in, and cursed shalt thou be when thou goest out.	Direction
7 The Lord shall cause thine enemies that rise up against thee to be smitten before thy face: they shall come out against thee one way, and flee before thee seven ways	25 The Lord shall cause thee to be smitten before thine enemies: thou shalt go out one way against them, and flee seven ways before them: and shalt be removed into all the kingdoms of the earth.	Opposers and enemies -war
8 The Lord shall command the blessing upon thee in thy storehouses, and in all that thou settest thine hand unto;	20 The Lord shall send upon thee cursing, vexation, and rebuke, in all that thou settest thine hand unto for to do, until thou be destroyed, and until thou perish quickly; because of the wickedness of thy doings, whereby thou hast forsaken me.	Action and endeavors
8b ...and he shall bless thee in the land which the Lord thy God giveth thee.	21 The Lord shall make the pestilence cleave unto thee, until he have consumed thee from off the land, whither thou goest to possess it.	Dwelling place
9 The Lord shall establish thee an holy people unto himself, as he hath sworn unto thee, if thou shalt keep the commandments of the Lord thy God, and walk in his ways.		Sanctified to God Set apart and revered by men
10 And all people of the earth shall see	37 And thou shalt become an	

Chapter 5 -Chart 2

Chapter 5 - The Two Consequences- the Binary Code of Blessing and Curses		
that thou art called by the name of the Lord; and they shall be afraid of thee.	astonishment, a proverb, and a byword, among all nations whither the Lord shall lead thee	
11 And the Lord shall make thee plenteous in goods, in the fruit of thy body, and in the fruit of thy cattle, and in the fruit of thy ground, in the land which the Lord sware unto thy fathers to give thee.	38 Thou shalt carry much seed out into the field, and shalt gather but little in; for the locust shall consume it. 39 Thou shalt plant vineyards, and dress them, but shalt neither drink of the wine, nor gather the grapes; for the worms shall eat them. 40 Thou shalt have olive trees throughout all thy coasts, but thou shalt not anoint thyself with the oil; for thine olive shall cast his fruit.	
12 The Lord shall open unto thee his good treasure, the heaven to give the rain unto thy land in his season, and to bless all the work of thine hand	23 And thy heaven that is over thy head shall be brass, and the earth that is under thee shall be iron. 24 The Lord shall make the rain of thy land powder and dust: from heaven shall it come down upon thee, until thou be destroyed.	Harvest or drought1
12b : and thou shalt lend unto many nations, and thou shalt not borrow. 13 And the Lord shall make thee the head, and not the tail; and thou shalt be above only, and thou shalt not be beneath; if that thou hearken unto the commandments of the Lord thy God, which I command thee this day, to observe and to do them:	43 The stranger that is within thee shall get up above thee very high; and thou shalt come down very low. 44 He shall lend to thee, and thou shalt not lend to him: he shall be the head, and thou shalt be the tail.	
	36 The Lord shall bring thee, and thy king which thou shalt set over thee, unto a nation which neither thou nor thy fathers have known; and there shalt thou serve other gods, wood and stone. .	exalted
	22 The Lord shall smite thee with a consumption, and with a fever, and with an inflammation, and with an extreme burning, and with the sword, and with blasting, and with mildew; and they shall pursue thee until thou perish.	Sickness and plague

Chapter 5 -Chart 3

Chapter 5 - The Two Consequences- the Binary Code of Blessing and Curses		
	26 And thy carcase shall be meat unto all fowls of the air, and unto the beasts of the earth, and no man shall fray them away.	Death
	27 The Lord will smite thee with the botch of Egypt, and with the emerods, and with the scab, and with the itch, whereof thou canst not be healed.	Skin desease
	28 The Lord shall smite thee with madness, and blindness, and astonishment of heart: 34 So that thou shalt be mad for the sight of thine eyes which thou shalt see.	Madness (mental illness) Blindness (Physical and spiritual) Fear and heart issues!
	29 And thou shalt grope at noonday, as the blind gropeth in darkness, and thou shalt not prosper in thy ways: and thou shalt be only oppressed and spoiled evermore, and no man shall save thee.	
	30 Thou shalt betroth a wife, and another man shall lie with her: thou shalt build an house, and thou shalt not dwell therein: thou shalt plant a vineyard, and shalt not gather the grapes thereof.	
	31 Thine ox shall be slain before thine eyes, and thou shalt not eat thereof: thine ass shall be violently taken away from before thy face, and shall not be restored to thee: thy sheep shall be given unto thine enemies, and thou shalt have none to rescue them.	
	32 Thy sons and thy daughters shall be given unto another people, and thine eyes shall look, and fail with longing for them all the day long; and there shall be no might in thine hand.	
	33 The fruit of thy land, and all thy labours, shall a nation which thou knowest not eat up; and thou shalt be only oppressed and crushed alway:	
	38 Thou shalt carry much seed out	

Chapter 5 -Chart 4

Chapter 5 - The Two Consequences- the Binary Code of Blessing and Curses		
	into the field, and shalt gather but little in; for the locust shall consume it. 39 Thou shalt plant vineyards, and dress them, but shalt neither drink of the wine, nor gather the grapes; for the worms shall eat them. 40 Thou shalt have olive trees throughout all thy coasts, but thou shalt not anoint thyself with the oil; for thine olive shall cast his fruit.	
	41 Thou shalt beget sons and daughters, but thou shalt not enjoy them; for they shall go into captivity.	
	42 All thy trees and fruit of thy land shall the locust consume.	
	45 Moreover all these curses shall come upon thee, and shall pursue thee, and overtake thee, till thou be destroyed; because thou hearkenedst not unto the voice of the Lord thy God, to keep his commandments and his statutes which he commanded thee: 46 And they shall be upon thee for a sign and for a wonder, and upon thy seed for ever.	
***Binary Contrasts* of Blessing and Curses**		
Increase or enlarge or add	Decrease or remove	
Prosper	Decline	
Succeed	Fail	
Gain	Loose	
Praise and honor	Vilification and dishonor	
To enrich	poverty	
Happiness	sorrow	

Chapter 5 -Chart 5

Three Blessings in the Bible	

The Aaronic Blessing - (Also known as the Priestly Blessing)		
"Speak to Aaron and his sons, saying, Thus you shall bless the people of Israel: you shall say to them:		**The Aaronic Blessing** ***Numbers 6:23-26*** **Hebrew meaning**
*'The Lord **bless** thee,*	**Sanctification**	"Barak" to bless, to endue with power for success.
*and **keep** thee:'*	**Protection**	"Samar" to exercise great care over as a Shepherd and protect!
*'The Lord make his **face** shine upon thee,*	**Favor**	"Paniym" face -meaning attention
*and be **gracious** unto thee:*	**Grace**	"Hanan" to be gracious or merciful
*The Lord **lift up his countenance** upon thee,*	**Redemption**	"nasa paniym" to lift up, to bear or carry away (sin)
*and give thee **peace**!*	**Peace**	"Shalom" peace, security and wholeness

The Ephesian Blessing - (Paul's prayer of blessing over the Ephesians)	
"I pray that He may grant you, according to the riches of His glory, to be strengthened with power in the inner man through His Spirit, and that the Messiah may dwell in your hearts through faith. I pray that you, being rooted and firmly established in love, may be able to comprehend with all the saints what is the length and width, height and depth of God's love, and to know the Messiah's love that surpasses knowledge, so you may be filled with all the fullness of God. Now to Him who is able to do above and beyond all that we ask or think according to the power that works in us!"	Ephesians 3:16-20: (HCSB)

The Galatians Blessing - (Paul's prayer of blessing over the Ephesians)	
"For this reason, also, since the day we heard this, we haven't stopped praying for you. We are asking that you may be filled with the knowledge of His will in all wisdom and spiritual understanding, so that you may walk worthy of the Lord, fully pleasing to Him, bearing fruit in every good work and growing in the knowledge of God. May you be strengthened with all power, according to His glorious might, for all endurance and patience, with joy giving thanks to the Father, who has enabled you to share in the saints' inheritance in the light. He has rescued us from the domain of darkness and transferred us into the kingdom of the Son He loves. We have redemption, the forgiveness of sins, in Him."	Colossians 1:9-14 (HCSB)

Chapter 5 -Chart 6

Matt.5:3-12-**The Beatitudes** – ***Jesus' Blessings for Suffering***	
CONTRAST OF ***SUFERINGS with REWARDS***	
3 Blessed are **the poor in spirit:**	for theirs is **the kingdom of heaven.**
4 Blessed are **they that mourn:**	for they **shall be comforted.**
5 Blessed are **the meek**:	for they **shall inherit the earth.**
6 Blessed are **they which do hunger and thirst after righteousness**:	for they **shall be filled.**
7 Blessed are **the merciful:**	for they **shall obtain mercy.**
8 Blessed are **the pure in heart:**	for they **shall see God.**
9 Blessed are **the peacemakers:**	for they **shall be called the children of God.**
10 Blessed are **they which are persecuted for righteousness' sake**:	for theirs is **the kingdom of heaven.**
11 Blessed are ye, **when men shall revile you, and persecute you, and shall say all** manner of evil against you falsely, for my sake	. 12 **Rejoice**, and be exceeding **glad**: for **great is your reward in heaven**

The Binary mountains – Mount Gerizim and Mount Ebal		
BLESSING	**CURSE**	
Mount Gerizim	**Mt Ebal**	
Simeon, Levi, Judah, Issachar, Joseph, (The children of Jacob's lawful wives, Leah and Rachel) (**Levites** were in between mountains reading the law and pronouncing the blessings and curses!)	**Gad, Asher** (children by Zilpah the slave) **Dan, Naphtali** (sons of Bilhah the slave) **Reuben** (was cursed because he had sexual relations with Bilhah, his father's concubine.) **Zebulun (**Failed to drive out the Canaanites living in Kitron and Nahalol)	**Division of the Twelve Tribes if Israel** **Separation of the children of the free and children of the slave**
The Southern Kingdom (Judah)	**The Northern Kingdom (Israel)**	**The divided Kingdom**
Redeemed from the Curse	**Curse of the law**	
Law of the Spirit	***Law of the Flesh***	Contrast of

Chapter 5 -Chart 7

"But if ye be **led of the Spirit**, ye are **not under the law**." Gal. 5:18	"**Therefore by the deeds of the law there shall no flesh be justified** in his sight: for by the law is the knowledge of sin." Romans 3:20	flesh and Spirit
Love fulfills the law "Therefore **love** is the **fulfillment of the law**." Rom. 13:8-10	***Flesh fails the Law*** For what **the law** was **powerless** to do because it was **weakened by the flesh**, Romans 8:3	God's Nature (Love) Vs Sin Nature
The Blessing and Curses of the tongue! Analogies of speech and the tongue		
Blessing of the Tongue ***Curse of the Tongue***	*" out of the same mouth proceedeth **blessing** and **cursing**"*	*James 3:10*
*"Therewith **bless we God**, even the Father; and therewith **curse we men**,"*	*Used for good and evil*	*James 3:9*
Bitter water	Sweet water	*James 3:11*
Salt water	Fresh water	*James 3:12*
Rudder to a ship	Small but directs a large ship	*James 3:4*
Fire	A small fire consumes much	*James 3:5,6*
Defiles the whole body		*James 3:6*
Untamable unlike animals	Bits in Horses mouths but not mans	*James 3:2,7,8*
Unruly evil		*James 3:8*
Full of deadly poison		*James 3:8*

Chapter 6 -Chart 1

Chapter Six- **The Two Covenants** - The Binary Code of the God's Law		
The Two Testaments		
The Old Testament (*Covenant*)	The New Covenant (*Covenant*)	
Abrahamic Covenant ." *Gen 17:5-9* **-Between Abraham and his seed (Israel)** **-Promised the land of Canaan**	***Covenant in Christ*** *Jer. 31:31-34* *Matt. 26:28* **Promised redemption & eternal life** **Promised abode in heaven**	Both Covenants of Promise Both Everlasting Covenants Both Conditional on Obedience
Abraham and Sarah to give birth in their old age	Virgin to give birth to Messiah	God's Sign of the Covenant (Miracle to confirm covenant)
Circumcision of the Flesh *Gen. 14:10-13*	Circumcision of the heart *Rom. 2:29, Eze 36:26*	Man's Sign of the Covenant
Abraham Believed God *Gen. 15:6, Gal. 3:6*	Those who believe in Christ *Eph. 2:8,9, Rom. 3:28, Acts 16:31*	Faith required
Heart of Stone (the Law)	Heart of flesh (love)	Two contrary hearts
Obedience to Mosaic Law	Law written in the heart (conscience)	
Ten commandments Law	Two Commandments Love (*Love fulfilleth the Law)* *Rom. 13:8-10*	Law given through Moses And Law given through Christ!
The Law of Sin and Death	The Law of the Spirit	*Rom. 8:22*
JACOB	**ISAAC**	Types of the Two Covenants
Son of Servant Hagar and Abraham	Son of Sarah & Abraham	Ismael removed so that Isaac could receive the inheritance
Son of Adoption	Natural Son of Promise	
Bondage	Freedom	
Mt Sinai *(where Law was given)* City of Jerusalem (Men in bondage)	Hill of Golgotha *(place of Crucifixion enabling Grace)* New Jerusalem (men are free)	
Covenant given only to Israel	Covenant given to the world	New Covenant superior *(Heb. 8:6, 7:22)*
Law (Works)	Grace	*Romans 6:14*
Works of the Law	Faith in Jesus Christ	Justification *Gal.2:16*

Chapter 7 -Chart 1

Chapter Seven- **The Two Positions** - The Binary Code of Truth and Error		
The Contrasts of Truth vs Error (lies and deception)		
TRUTH	**ERROR**	
Unalterable, unchanging, eternal	Contrary, Manipulated, distorted	*Rom. 1:18,24*
Pure	**Diluted**	
Absolute	**Deniable**	
Jesus is the Truth *John 14:6*, *John 1:14* God never lies *Num. 23:19* *Tit. 1:12*	-Satan is Father of Lies -There is no Truth in him -Lying is his native language *John 8:44*	
Gods people walk in Truth	Sinners walks in Deception	*"For I rejoiced greatly when brethren came and testified of the* ***truth*** *that is in you, just as* ***you walk in the truth****. I have no greater joy than to hear that my children* ***walk in truth.****"* **3 John 3-4**.
Truth sets you free *(John 8:23, 31,32)*	**Refusing the truth entraps one into deception!** *1 John 1:8*	
God's word is truth *Psalm 86:11, Psalm 119:160* Jesus words are Truth *John 17:17, John 18:37-38*	Satan's words are false	
Spirit of truth	Spirit of Error	*1 John 4:6*
Grace and Truth came through Jesus	The Law came through Moses	*1 John 1:17*
True Worship in Spirit and Truth *John 4:24*	False Worship is religious and erroneous!	True vs Counterfeit worship *John 4:19-26*
Holy Spirit called the Spirit of Truth *John 16:13*	Antichrist full of deception *2 Thess. 2:8-12*	
The Truth sanctifies us and makes us holy! *John 17:17*	Lying lips are an abomination to the Lord! *Prov. 12:22*	
We preach a message of truth *Eph. 1:13,14*	Message of truth hidden from unbelievers. *2 Cor. 4:3-4*	
Those who belong to God hear the truth	Those who belong to God do not hear the truth	*John 8:47*
Truth is eternal	Lies are temporary	*Pro. 12:19*
Faithful witness speaks truth	False witness lies	*Pro. 14:5, Eph. 4:15*
Truth opens our eyes	Lies blinds us to the truth	*2 Cor. 4:3-4, John 9:39*
Holy Spirit and <u>Power</u> *"Dunimus: Force, ability and might"*	<u>Power</u> of the Devil *"katadunasteuw: Dominion or oppression"*	*Acts 10:38 NIV*

Chapter 8 -Chart 1

Chapter Eight-Accuse or Excuse! The Binary Code of our Conscience		
Binary Conscience		
Good Conscience- Right	**Guilty Conscience-Wrong**	
Excusing us	Accusing us	Romans 2:15
Inner spirit Bears witness		1 John 3:18
Law written in our hears		Pro. 20:27
Love from a pure heart		1 Tim. 1:19
Sincere faith	Shipwrecked faith	
Listens to voice of Conscience	Ignores voice of Conscience	Acts 28:27
	Heart id calloused	
	Conscience Defiled	Titus 1:15
	Conscience Seared (cauterized)	1 Tim. 4:2
Heart of Flesh	Heart of Stone	
Clear conscience		Acts 24:16, Heb. 13:18, 1 Tim. 3:9
Eternal Clear Conscience	Temporary Clear Conscience	
Jesus Sacrifice	Jewish sacrifices	
Blood of Jesus	Blood of Calf and Goats	Heb. 9:12-14
Baptism a sign of Good conscience		1 Peter 3:21

Chapter 9-Chart 1

Chapter Nine-The Two Realms – The Binary Code of the Spirit and Matter		
Binary Nature of Man		
Spiritual man	**Fleshly Man**	
Spirit/ soul	Physical body	
Inward Man	Outward Man	
Spiritual; Birth	Physical Birth	John 3:6
	War against the Soul	1 Pet. 2:11
	War against the Mind	
Contrary to each other	Conflicts with each other	Gal. 5:17
Walk in the Spirit	Walk in the Flesh	Rom. 8:3-9, Gal 5:16
Mind on the spirit is Peace	Mind on the Flesh is Death	
Inner spirit Beats witness	Hostile to God	
Law written in our hears	does not submit to God	
Spirit rules over the Flesh	Flesh rules over the Spirit	
	Can not please God	Rom. 8:8
	Works of the Flesh	Gal. 5:19, Col. 3:5-8
Fruit of the Spirit		Gal. 5:22-25
The New Man	**The Old Man**	
Righteous and Holy	Corrupt	Eph. 4:22
New Creation	Sinful nature	2 Cor. 5:17
Binary Nature of Christians		
The Spiritual Man	**The Carnal Man**	
Spiritual (Mature)	Babes in Christ (immature)	1 Cor. 3:1-6
Meat of the Word	Milk of the word	1 Cor. 3:1-6, 1 Peter 2:2
	Envy, strife and division	1 Cor. 3:1-6
Spiritual Discerns	Perceives not the things of the Spirit	1 Cor. 2:14
Binary Bodies	At His coming	
Glorified Bodies	**Fleshly Bodies**	
Incorruptible	Corruptible	1 Cor. 15:51-54
Spiritual and Physical realm	Limited to Physical realm	
Body redeemed		Rom. 8:23
Immortal	Mortal	1 Cor. 1"10
Absent from Body- present with the Lord	Separated from God	1 Cor. 5:8

Chapter 10 -Chart 1

Chapter Ten- The Two Orders- The Binary Code of God's Priesthood		
Binary Priesthood		
Aaronic Priesthood	**Melchizedek Priesthood**	*Two orders- Intercessors for Man*
Descendants of Aaron and sons	Appointed by God	
I will be with thy mouth, and with his mouth		*Ministry of Priest to the people*
He will teach you what ye shall do		Exo. 4:14-16
He shall be thy spokesman unto the people		
	First mention of Priest in Bible	
Earthly, Temporary Priest	Heavenly, Eternal Priest	Heb. 7:14-17, Heb. 6:20
Binary Priesthood divided		
Faithful Priesthood	**Corrupt Priesthood**	
Eleazar and Ithamar	Nadab and Abihu	
Was obedient to Moses	Offered up "Strange Fire"	Lev. 10:6-7, Exo.. 30:9
Lived and descendants became priesthood	Died by fire and lost lineage of priesthood	
Aaronic priests	**Levitical priests**	
Descendants of Eleazar and Ithamar (Levites)	Descendants of tribe of Levite!	
Duties of Sanctuary and altar	Duties of maintaining the tent of meeting	Num. 18:4-5
Received offering from the people.	Received tithes and cities rather than land!	Num. 18:2, Num. 18:8-19
Ministered in the Tabernacle in wilderness	took down and set up Tabernacle.	Numbers 1:51
Ministered in Spiritual things	Ministered in physical things	Numbers 1:50
Type of Elders or Bishops in the Church	Type of Deacons n the Church	Acts 6:1
High Priest – Chief Priest	**Priest**	Lev. 21
Only one allowed into Holy of Holies	Allowed in Holy place, not Holy of Holies	Lev. 16:29:30
Offered sacrifice on Day of atonement	offered sacrifice all year	Lev. 16:24
Bring Incense into the Holy of Holies		Lev. 16:12-13
Sprinkled Blood on the Mercy seat		Lev. 16:15, Heb 9:7
A Type of Christ		Hebrews 9:12-14
A type of Presiding Elder (Later Pastor)		

Chapter 10 -Chart 2

Chapter Ten- The Two Orders- The Binary Code of God's Priesthood		
Binary Priesthood divided in New Testament		
Pharasees	**Sadducees**	
Believed in ressurrection	Did not Believe in Resurrection	Acts 23:8
	No afterlife or Hell	
	No rewards or punishment	
Believed in Spirits and Angels	Did not believe in Spirits or Angels	Acts 23:8
Popular with most of the people	Popular with elitists and the aristocrats	
Religious Divisions in the Church		
Jewish believers	Gentile Believers	Acts 6, Acts 2:11-21
Protestants	Catholics	
Binary Ministry of Melchezedek		
Priest	**King**	
Tithe given by Abraham	Melchezadek means "righteous King	
"Priest of the most high God!"	King of Salem (Jerusalem)	Genesis 14:18
Ministers to the people	Rules the people with righteousness	Jer. 23:5
Offered Prayers ans petitions for mankind		Hebrews 5:6-10

Chapter 11 -Chart 1

Chapter Eleven- Remembering and Forgetting- The Binary Code of Memory!		
Binary Memory		
Remembering	Forgetting	Good or Bad
Recalling the Past	Releasing the past	Always deals with the Past
affects present and future	Prone to repeat same mistakes	
Gods Faithfulness in the past		Isaiah 46: 8-10
Prophets spoke to help Israel Remember		Eze. 36:31
Jewish parents to teach Children so they would not forget what He has done		Deut. 11:2, 19-21
Jewish Feasts as Memorials to help remember		Deut. 16:3
Sabbath a memorial to remember rest		Exo. 20:8
Jesus instructs Disciples to remember his words		Mark 8:18, John 16:2-4
	Paul puts his past behind him	Phil.3:13-14
	Old life passed away	Phil. 2:13
	God forgets our sins	Jer.31:34, Isa. 43:25
Book of Remembrance- works and sins?	Book of Life-Name Blotted out	Mal. 3:16, Ex. 32:32

Chapter 12 -Chart 1

Chapter Twelve- The Two Adams -The Binary Code of Redemption		
Binary Code of Sin vs Salvation		
First man Adam	**Second Adam -Jesus**	
A Living Being	A Life Giving Spirit	1 Cor. 15:44,45
Populated Earth	Populates Heaven	
Likeness of Adam	Likeness of Christ	
Sin passed on to mankind	Forgiveness given to believers	Rom. 5:12, Acts 4:12
Sin came by disobedience	Salvation came by obedience	Rom. 5:17-21
Adam brought death to all mankind	Jesus died for all mankind	Phil. 28
First with physical body	First with resurrected spiritual body	1 Cor. 46-49
Binary Bodies		
Physical Bodies	**Spiritual Resurrected bodies**	
The Seed	The Tree	1 Cor. 15:35-38, Matt.13:31-32
natural Body	spiritual body	
Earthly Man	Heavenly Man	1 Cor:15:46-49
Limited to Physical Realm	Physical and Spiritual Realm	
Son of Man (Son of Adam)	**Son of God**	
The Word made Flesh	Part of Godhead	1 John 1:14, Col. 2:9
Term for Messiah		Dan. 7:13,14
Stephen's testimony of Messiah		Acts 7:55-58
Jesus Testimony of being the Messiah		Matt.12:8, 13:41, 18:11, Mark 10,
		Luke 9:22, John 5:27, Mark 14:62
	Gods' Testimony of his Son	Matt. 3:17, Matt. 17;5
Binary brides		
Bride of First Adam	**Bride of Second Adam (Bride of Christ)**	
Eve – the Mother of all Living	The Church	Eph. 5:3
Made from Adam's Body	Made from Adam's seed	
Union of Marriage	Wedding feast in Heaven	Rev. 18:7-9, 19:9
Love your wives	Christ loves the Church and gave himself	Eph. 5:25-27

Chapter 13 -Chart 1

Chapter Thirteen- The Lamb and the Lion- The Binary Code of Messiah		
Binary Mission of Messiah		
The Lamb of God	**The Lion of the Tribe of Judah**	
Jesus the Lamb	Jesus the Lion	Rev. 5: 4-7
Humble, gentle, sacrificial	Strong, might, bold and conquering	Two Natures
First as sacrifice for Sins	Second to reign and rule	Two Comings Acts 1:9
Testimony of John the Baptist		John 1:29
Testimony of Isaiah		Isa. 53:2-12
Lamb is worthy		Rev. 5:12-14
Redeemed by the Blood of the Lamb		1 Peter 1:18-20
Prepared before earths foundations laid		1 Peter 1:18-20
	Will return to fight the nations	Zec. 14:3-4
	Will judge the nations & all people	Isa. 1:5,10
	Shall rule as King over the earth	Gen. 49:10, John 12:12-16, Rev. 19:14-16

Chapter 14 -Chart 1

Chapter Fourteen- Worldliness and Holiness- The Binary Code of Influence		
Binary Influence		
Worldliness	**Holiness**	
The World, the Flesh and the Devil	The Father, Son and Holy Spirit	Trinities of influence/ 1 John 2:16, 1 John 5:7
The lust of the Eyes, the Flesh and Pride		1 John 2:15-17
World hate Jesus and his followers		John 15:18-19, John 17:14-16
Be not conformed	Be transformed	Rom. 12:2
Influence– Compromise -Assimilation	Holiness	1 Pet.1:15-16 Heb. 12:14, 2 Cor. 7:1
Sin of Balaam		Jude 11, Numbers 31:14,16, Joshua 13:22
	Set apart to God	Lev.20:26
The World	**The Kingdom of God**	
	Not of this World	John 18:36
Love not the world or things in the world	Set affections on High	1 John 2:15-17

Chapter 15 -Chart 1

Chapter Fifteen- Religion vs Relationship – the Code of the Pursuit of God		
Binary Religion		
Human Religion	**Christianity**	
Outward knowledge	Personal relationship	Matt. 23:27 / John 14:6
Mans **reverence** to God	Gods **revelation** to Man	Acts 4:12
Man efforts to know God	Jesus way to God the father	Acts 14:12, 1 John 2:23
Form of Godliness	**True Godliness**	2 Tim. 3:5
Denying the Power	Sanctified by Holy Spirit	2 Tim. 3:5
Outward condition	internal condition	Matthew 23:28, Mark 12:38-40
Pride, Pandering & Pretense	Humble, Pleasing God & genuine	1 Pet 5:6
Self effort, false piety	Conformed and transformed into the image of Christ	Rom.8:29, 2 Cor. 3:18
Man Pleasers	**God Pleasers**	
appeases God	pleasing God	Gal. 1:10, Col. 10
Will reap man's reward	Will reap God's reward	John 5:41, Matt. 6:1
Obeys man	Obeys God	Acts 5:29
Seeks man's approval	Seeks God's approval	John 12:43, 1 Thess. 2:4
Seeks man's Favor	Seeks God's will	Eph. 6:6
justified in Man's eyes	justified in God's eyes	Luke 16:15
Highly esteemed by man	Detestable by God	Luke 16:15

Chapter 16 -Chart 1

Chapter Sixteen- The Beginning and the end – The Binary Code of Time		
Binary Time vs Eternity		
The Beginning	**The end**	In contrast to eternity
Time created by God for man	Eternity is God's realm	
Governed by heavenly bodies	Governed by God's nature	
Time is temporary	Eternity is forever	
Time is a stop watch	Time has expiration date	
In the Beginning started time	time will end and eternity takes over	
Genesis a type of the beginning	Revelation a type of the end	
Individual lives is a allotment of time	Eternal life is a gift of God	Heb. 9:27, John 3:16
Birth – the Beginning of life	Death the End of life	
Seconds, minutes, hours, years	events, actions, experiences	Man and God's measurements of time
Linear time, sequential	Cyclical, repeatable	
Purpose of time: to man it is ti live	To God it is to learn and come to know Him!	2 Peter 3:9
Time to man is about Pleasure	To God it is Purpose and Accountability	2 Cor.5:10
Time	**Eternity**	
Temporary	Forever	
Finite	Infinite	
Physical realm (Things seen)	Spiritual realm (Things unseen)	1 Cor. 4:18
Visible	Invisible	
Earth and heavens (universe)	New heavens and new earth	Isa. 65:17, 2 Pet 3:13
Two Destructions:water/fire		2 Pet 3:5-12
Earth created and destroyed by Gods voice		Heb. 12:26-27
Chaos and disunity	God unifies everything	Eph. 1:9-10
The Alpha	**The Omega**	Jesus
The Beginning	The end	Rev. 12:13
The First	The Last	Rev. 12:13
He encompasses all time – He who was (past) who is (present) and is to come (future) Rev. 1:8		
He created Time	He will end Time	Rev. 21:4-6
Word was made flesh- The eternal entered the fabric of time		John 1:14

Chapter 17 -Chart 1

Chapter Seventeen- Punishments and Rewards – The Binary Code of Judgment		
Binary Code of Judgment and Rewards		
Punishment /Judgment	**Reward**	
All actions have consequences		
God executes judgment		Psa.75:6-7
No action is hidden from God		Mark 4:22
Some actions are judged in this life and some at the throne room of God		1 Tim.5:24
Eternal separation from God	Eternal life in the presence of God	2 Thess. 1:9, Matt 25:46
Sowing	**Reaping**	Gal 6:7
Sowing to the flesh	Reaps corruption	Gal. 6:8
Sowing to the spirit	Reaps eternal Life	Gal. 6:8-9
Good or bad seed	Produces good or bad fruit	Action = results
sparingly or generously	sparingly or generously	2 Cor.9:6, Luke 6:38
Good ground	**Bad ground**	Matt. 13:1-23, Mark 4:1-20, Luke 8:4-15
30, 60 and 100 fold	Wayside, Rocky ground, Thorny ground	Word multiplies or word dies
growth	no growth	
The seed, the blade and full corn	No maturity	levels of maturity, Mark 4:26-29
Fruitfulness	Unfruitful	
Tree and fruit good	Tree and fruit bad	Matt. 12:33
Receptive hearts	Unreceptive hearts	
Judgment of words	**Binary Resurections**	Jesus alone is Judge of all man
Out of the Abundance of the heart the mouth speaks		Matt.12:34
Good man, good treasure, good things	Evil man, evil treasure, evil things	Matt. 12:35,36
Words will Justify and acquit	Words will condem	
Holy Spirit convicts of sin & judgment	Holy Spirit will convict of righteousness	John 16:7-8
Resurrection of Judgment	Resurrection of Life	John 5:22-30
The Wicked	The Righteous	

Chapter 17 -Chart 2

Chapter Seventeen- Punishments and Rewards – The Binary Code of Judgment		
Jesus Parables of separation and judgment		
Kingdom of God	**Destruction**	
Sheep on right side	Goats on left side	Matt:25:31-34
The Wheat (good seed)	The Tares (sown by the enemy	Matt. 13:24-30
Wheat gathered to the owner's barn	Tares destroyed by fire	
The Good Fish	The Bad Fish	Matt. 13-47-50
The Prodigal Son	The Privileged Son	Luke 15:11-32
Humility and seeking forgiveness	Jealous and entitled	
the Unforgiven Servant	The Unforgiving servant or King's servant	The Two Servants – Matt. 18:32-35
The last who will be first	The first who will be last	The Parable of the Laborers
The Downcast	The Privileged	God's positional grace- Matt. 20:1-16
Obedient son	Disobedient son	The Two Sons
Said he would but did not obey his father	Said he wouldn't but obeyed his father	
Faithful Servant	The Wicked Servant	Matt. 24:45-51
The Wise Man	The Foolish Man	Matt. 7:24-27
Two Births	**Two Deaths**	Binary code of life and death
Physical Birth of water		John 3:1-10
Spiritual Birth of the Spirit		
	Physical death -soul from body	Rev.2:10, 21:8
	Spiritual death -soul from God	
	Death and Hell in Lake of fire	Rev. 20:13,14
Resurrection of Life	**Resurrection of Judgment**	Binary resurrections
Those who have done good	Those who have done evil	John 5:28
The just	the unjust	Acts:24:15
Some raised at the rapture		1 Thess. 4:13-18
Some at his second coming (martyrs and believers during the tribulation)		Rev. 20:4-6
Book of Life	**Book(s) of Remembrance**	The Two Books – Binary evidence for Judgment
The Righteous	The Wicked	Malachi 3:16-18, Rev. 20:11-12
Names written in Book of Life		Rev. 13:8, Rev.20:14,15, Rev 10:20,
	Names Blotted out of Book of Life	Psa. 69:27-28, Rev. 3:5,6, 2 Cor. 5:10

Chapter 18 -Chart 1

Chapter Eighteen- Summary		
The Binary Code of the old and New Systems		
The World System	**The Kingdom of God**	
Old creation	New creation	2 Cor. 5:17, Rev 21:5
Heaven and earth	New heaven and Earth	Revelation 21:1.
Temporary	Eternal life in the presence of God	1 Cor. 4:18
Tainted and defiled	Pure and Holy	Isa. 24:5, Rev. 21:27
Worldly Sorrow	The Joy of the Lord	2 Cor. 7:9-10, Rom. 14:17
Isolation and separation	Eternal fellowship	Matt 25:32. 1 John 1:3, Rev 21:3-4
Struggle and hardship	Enter into His Rest	John 16:33, Isaiah 57:1-2
Ban from Garden	Welcomed into his Paradise	Gen. 3:22-23 Rev. 2:7
Ban from Tree of Life	Can now eat freely from Tree of life	Gen. 3:22-23 Rev. 2:7
Dusty, dirty roads	Pure golden Streets	Matt. 10:11-14, Rev. 21,21
Curses and restrictions	Blessing and Abundance	Psa. 37:22
Night time and Darkness	Light of Christ	Acts 26:18, John 8:12

About the Author

Gerald (Jerry) Lee Wall has been a Christian for over 50 years. He got saved at 17 through a supernatural experience and spent the 70's and 80's as an evangelist street preaching and hitchhiking across the country preaching the gospel. He was a counselor at Explo 72, a large Billy Graham crusade in Dallas, Texas

Jerry went on to function as a teacher in the eighties and later was an Pastor in Miami, Florida and an Associate Pastor in Ft Lauderdale, Florida. He later moved to Georgia and began to function prophetically in his local church. He is now retired after spending over 40 years in the printing and publishing business as well as a freelance graphic designer. Jerry is married and has 4 daughters and eight grandchildren!

Printed in Great Britain
by Amazon

17790580R00108